Barcode in Back

MW00380356

A Music Producer's Thoughts to Create By

By Keith Olsen

HUMBER LIBRARIES LAKESHORE CAMPUS
3199 Lakeshore Blvd West
TORONTO, ON.   M8V 1K8

THOMSON

COURSE TECHNOLOGY

Professional ■ Technical ■ Reference

HUMBER LIBRARIES LAKESHORE CAMPUS
3199 Lakeshore Blvd West
TORONTO, ON.   M8V 1K8

A Music Producer's Thoughts to Create By

©2006 by Keith Olsen. All rights reserved. No part of this book may be reproduced or transmitted in
any form or by any means, electronic or mechanical, including photocopying, recording, or by any information storage or retrieval system
without written permission from Thomson Course Technology PTR, except for the inclusion of brief quotations in a review.

The ArtistPro and Thomson Course Technology PTR logos and related trade dress are trademarks of
Thomson Course Technology PTR and may not be used without written permission.

All other trademarks are the property of their respective owners.

Cover photo: Counterpoint Studios, Salt Lake City, ©Scot Zimmerman, studio design by studio bau:ton.

Publisher and General Manager, Thomson Course Technology PTR: Stacy L. Hiquet

Associate Director of Marketing: Sarah O'Donnell

Manager of Editorial Services: Heather Talbot

Marketing Manager: Mark Hughes

Executive Editor: Mike Lawson

Copywriter: Cathleen D. Snyder

Marketing Coordinator: Jordan Casey

Project Editor & Copy Editor: Brian Proffitt

Technical Editor: Glenn Lorbecki

Thomson Course Technology PTR Editorial Services Coordinator: Elizabeth Furbish

Cover Designer & Interior Layout Tech: Stephen Ramirez

Illustrator: Danilo Bonilla

Indexer: Larry D. Sweazy

Proofreader: Laura R. Gabler

Important: Thomson Course Technology PTR cannot provide software support. Please contact the
appropriate software manufacturer's technical support line or Web site for assistance.

Thomson Course Technology PTR and the author have attempted throughout this book to distinguish proprietary trademarks
from descriptive terms by following the capitalization style used by the manufacturer.

Information contained in this book has been obtained by Thomson Course Technology PTR from sources believed to be reliable.
However, because of the possibility of human or mechanical error by our sources, Thomson Course Technology PTR, or others,
the Publisher does not guarantee the accuracy, adequacy, or completeness of any information and is not responsible for any
errors or omissions or the results obtained from use of such information. Readers should be particularly aware of the fact that
the Internet is an ever-changing entity. Some facts may have changed since this book went to press.

Educational facilities, companies, and organizations interested in multiple copies or licensing of this book should contact
the Publisher for quantity discount information. Training manuals, CD-ROMs, and portions of this book are
also available individually or can be tailored for specific needs.

ISBN: 1-59200-985-9
Library of Congress Catalog Card Number: 2005929803

Printed in the United States
06 07 08 09 10 PH 10 9 8 7 6 5 4 3 2 1

Thomson Course Technology PTR, a division of Thomson Course Technology
25 Thomson Place
Boston, MA 02210
www.courseptr.com

This book is dedicated to all who put in the time and energy to perfect their art and understand that there are no quick and easy paths. And finally to those who realize there isn't a talent plug-in—success only comes with hard work and practice.

Contents

Introduction

This book was written to inspire dedication to fully developing your Potential. You never know where or when an idea, story, or melody will come to you. The creative flow is within all of us. It is the harnessing of that energy; the fulfillment of our dream is what drives us all to get into this industry in the first place.

While the Potential is within us all, it comes down to how we focus this energy and how we utilize this promise that really counts. It is always best to have tried than to fear failure. There is no luck here, just infinite dedication to one's art. The more dedicated you are, the better your chances. Let this book guide you and be a source of sanity, reason, and experience.

The next section is probably the most important one you'll read in this book as it states the facts that determine how far you may go in your journey. Without a total understanding of these few paragraphs it could be pointless in continuing. Take your time and read the next page carefully, never invert or change the order of the three elements; they have not changed to this date, and I don't think they ever will.

The Three Elements That Are in All Hit Records

There are only 12 tones in Western music culture, and it's the way you arrange them that makes the difference and makes them unique. Within this process is this wonderful and meaningful collaboration between musicians, melody writers, lyricists, sound designers, producers, and engineers.

As you prepare to embark on your career, never forget that there are hundreds (actually thousands) of others out there that are doing the same thing. Put your best foot forward. Don't fill a CD with 10 or 20 songs in hope that one of them will catch someone's ear. The people you'll send these songs to just don't have the time, and you should not expect them to even listen to the entire collection you assemble.

These rules are guidelines to help keep you focused. Your best efforts can always be heard if you follow a few simple rules. Make sure your creative process always includes:

▶ Great Song

▶ Great Performance of that song (this includes the arrangement)

▶ Great Sound (remember it's last on the list)

Part I

Song

CHAPTER 1

It's All About the Story

A song is storytelling put to a melody. I recall one July 4th holiday when a very well-known legendary songwriter once told me, "All your life, you carry around this bag on your shoulder, we'll call it the life experience bag. As you experience life and the wonders that revolve within it, you put these experiences in the bag. When you write, you reach down into this bag and pull them out, one at a time, but never get too comfortable that you don't keep putting stories back into the bag or else one day you'll dig in and there's nothing left but this old rotten apple core. And you know, nobody wants to hear a story about an old rotten apple core." Thanks Carole for those words of wisdom and advice.

Keep your mind clear and think of how you would like to have someone speak to you. It seems overly simple, doesn't it? However, it's easy to underestimate your ultimate customer, that listener out there in radioland.

Maintaining the listener's attention is harder than you think. Remind yourself of the place where most music is still heard by the masses. That's right, it's the car radio. There are so many distractions for drivers to take their attention away from your music. There are buses driving by, road signs, billboards, traffic, and people on the sidewalks. How do you keep their attention glued to your story?

When you tell the story, make sure the listener can understand it on the first pass. Don't be so bold as to think you have more than one pass to hook the listener; you probably don't have that much time. You want your listeners to "claim" your story as their own, with expressions such as "That's cool, I wish my life could be that," or "Wow, they're talkin' about me!" As you work your way through the story, make it short, concise and easy to understand. Don't worry about the rhyming scheme just yet. Be the storyteller.

This story can take on many faces. A film director once told me that everyone has a story, at least one story that is or can be told to other people and garner attention. This is probably true, although through the course of our lives we each see stories unfold in front of us all the time. It's how we retell this story that counts. This is an art. Great authors tell fictional stories that come to life out of a book and you see the scenes in full color in your mind. This is the quest we're looking for in a song. To enable the story to be understood throughout the song is a nifty trick. So many of the songs I've heard get disguised with production. Simplicity is really the name of the game. Think of this story as if it is with the last breath you take. What are you going to say? What do you want to leave behind for the world to know? Can you do it in one breath? Can you see how you really don't have much time?

This is a good test of the song's "hook." The hook in a song needs to be simple, a single thought, a single idea, and a single subject. It is important to not overcomplicate the story. Is the story about a guy meeting a girl? Then keep it about a guy meeting a girl. Find the words to generally describe this fact. This is where the clever statement overcomes complex elaboration.

Setting the Hook

Now that you've come to the understanding of how important that hook statement is, and you've found the words that excite the right emotion, proceed on with the finite explanation and conclusions of the story. See how you've set the bar pretty high? This is really a good thing. You have a level of justification to move forward.

Whether it's a day or month after you've completed any song and are on to the next one, always keep in mind the level of quality of your best song. All songs after your best song will be judged accordingly. Isn't this business wonderful? This is true if you are an aspiring or signed songwriter/artist, or even if you're a serious hobbyist. Once you've told a great story, all of your future stories need to be just as inspired.

Know your listener and write accordingly. The lyric within a story can be one of the hardest things to accomplish. Avoid those tricky buzzwords that you hear all the time today. I guarantee that you'll hate that part of your own lyric ten years from now if you use current catchphrases. Believe me, if this song is a hit and you are the performer, for the rest of your professional career you'll have to continue to play that song. Let it not be "that damn" song 10 years from now.

Implied rhythm of the lyric: it's more than just a rhyme, there is that internal clock, the pace, the accents on which part of a word's syllable. All of these combine to contribute greatly to the final presentation of your story. Look at the lyrics of many of your favorite hit songs, note how the story is told not just by words, but also by where in the phrase the accent falls:

You were on a liquid diet,
You were sure you had to try it
and you lost all your pounds

The doctor's on vacation,
So you took the medication
and wound up in lost and found

So we took a trip to Paris
cause you swore that it would scare us
out of our swift decline

All that I remember
`bout those days in that September
is the merci' and the wine

You talk on the telephone,
Long distance to New York or Rome
Some people say you got it made

Your home is like a fortress,
No one comes in but the florist
the gardener, and the maid

You call me on the telephone,
You say you feel so alone
too tired to get dressed and get out

First you're happy, then you're sad
somehow you always hang up mad
Excuse me if I shout
Precious Time, Precious Time, Precious Time
Copyright: Billy Steinberg used with permission

Hot blooded
Check it and see
I got a fever of 103
Hey baby, can you do more than dance
I'm hot blooded, hot blooded
Copyright Mick Jones, Lou Graham used with permission

Can it get much simpler? If you've always thought that more is better, well, think back to all the greatest hits that you have loved in the past and think of how simple they really were. The effect of the story is profound. To excite the listener, you must secure the immediacy of the story to be "owned" by the listener, more specifically to imply that the guy or girl sees or feels that they are a part of the story. They must be this part of it or be so into what's going to happen that their attention will not drift from the song.

Listener Ownership

If the listener has a bit of ownership into the song, if he thinks that the song directly relates to his life, then you are way ahead of the game. There are so many ways to accomplish this and there are no hard and fast rules, just helpful hints that will move you along. This hook into the ownership quirks of the listener can come many ways. Some are story related, some are melodic and yet others are those infectious arrangement hooks. Your best bet is in the presentation of the story. It is done by using clever paraphrasing, an idiosyncratic play on words, or setting up a catch phrase that is repeated at the end of almost each phrase lyrically. These are all ways to sell your story to the listener.

There is nothing more important in writing a great song. Selling is a part of your daily life. You sell yourself on the idea that you're a great artist/producer/writer/engineer. Now sell your customer, that person driving in the car and listening to the radio. Don't worry if you don't get a feeling of the melody or lyric across the first time or even the second or third time you read it back to yourself, this is common and underlines your dedication. Keep at it and you will find the way. *The storyline is the most important part of the song.* How many times have I stated that fact? Do not dismiss the importance of the story.

Try to not tell the same story that everyone's heard a thousand times before. I know that is the hard part since most songs are written about relationships. That said, with every relationship there is a genuine unique twist. That's the way I've seen it in my life. Earlier I showed the example of "That's cool, I wish my life could be that," or "Wow, they're talkin' about me!" With ownership it's the same game. Share ownership with the listener and you will have a real hook!

I once told an artist to write about a subject that has never been written about before, so what did he do? Well, he wrote a song about Chinese Food… clever when you read the lyrics:

I got my salad without no crouton,
I got my fig without no Newton,
I got my meat sliced real nice,
but what I really want is some fried rice…
Give me some Chinese Food…
Copyright 1990 Freddie Kagan

The Melody

You hear a song on the radio or on MTV and you just can't get it out of your head. Its melody was so infectious that you find yourself humming it, whistling it, you heard it only once, but there it is, still in your head. Usually you'll find that the melody is so simple it just stuck there. I heard an old Spin Doctors hit the other day and now I wake up with that melody in my head, I shower with it, drive with it. I never heard the tune that much when it was a hit, but now just one pass and it seems like it'll be in there forever. Finally that melody left my inner ear, but for the longest time it still lingered. This is the true melodic addiction that you should be striving for.

To find this melody, there are no rules or formulas to follow. Some say it's luck, while others say that it comes from thin air. I tend to agree with the latter. Where and when a melody will come to you is a mystery. This is part of the stealth, skunk-works kind of creative flow that we can't put our collective fingers on.

To say that you worked on a melody for a set of changes last night really means that you fiddled around until something sounded good to you. Is that songwriting? You bet it is. I worked with songwriters that have the gift where a melody will just come to them. They'll sing it for days on end. Then they try to put a structure and changes to it that make sense. Is this melody writing? Wow, I'd say it is!

Your state of mind is your best bet when dealing with melody. To sit back and see how others perceive this melody is another key. Do they grab onto the main elements or are they taken by the subtleties within? Do not make the melody so complex that it requires total concentration of the listener. Always stay on the edge of simplicity.

Where does the lyric want the melody to go? Let this be more of a source of inspiration and use it as a tool. Utilizing your lyric, as a tool in writing your melody, is one of the tricks I can help you with in this book. If the lyric gets tremendously somber then maybe the melody should be more somber in content. "No kidding," you say? Well, I can't tell you the number of times where I've heard melodies that start complex and try to wiggle around enough to project a story and in the end they have just confused me and anyone else who listen to it.

Structure without Structure

Structuring a melody need not be a formula; moreover it needs to be in a form that follows your structure or function. The old 1980s form of: Intro, verse 1, B section (or pre chorus), Chorus, repeat that whole line, and then go to an 8 bar bridge followed by the chorus 10 times is predictable but sometimes very usable. It's all about how you use common structure versus breaking the structure.

I spoke about that writer I've worked with that writes all melodies cold then fits them into a structure that works for the genre. This way of working has been very profitable for him, but to say it is *the* way to do it is ludicrous. Any way you can put across your melody is OK. This is when pure creativity starts rapidly flowing.

Where does the melody start within the new changes that are written? Move the start one beat or a tick or so later and see what happens. It can be very interesting. Melodies that fall across bar lines are always inventive.

This is what I mean about the structure of the song. When the chord changes on the bar line and the phrase starts a beat or two before or after, wow that can be cool! Doing some form of 3 against 4 phrasing can also be ingenious. This is your inspiration and it comes out of your heart, not out of any book.

Clever and Copying

When you simplify and or finalize your melody and structure, your composition might break a few rules, but you're happy with the outcome. Now after all the work, you have to qualify everything you've done by looking to see if you're walking that fine line between clever and copying.

Once again I reiterate, there are only 12 notes, so sooner or later you will unknowingly plagiarize from some copyright somewhere in the world. Fear not, if you are just writing your song, you'll have many parts of it that will not be of *"equal pitch and duration,"* as stated in the copyright laws. If you think you've heard that melody before, relax, you probably have! Go back to it another day and see if the part that sounds recognizable is really there and change it a bit.

Complexities Need Not Be Obvious

To simplify or to complicate, that is the true question. How many times have you wanted to put in a left turn in the melody that will twist the listener? You know it's really hard to be clever every time you try to do some form of left turn.

Complexities in melodies are just as problematic as in arrangements. For instance, let's say that the chorus is being a bit stagnant and that within a few bars the melody really soars. How about using something very complex here in this section? However, you don't need to necessarily do it with the melody, perhaps try using three-part background vocals. Maybe the fix is just in-between the lead vocal lines and is a complex harmonic swell that leads the listener to the next chord, keeping the listener glued to hear what happens next. There are complex usages of harmonic interludes that only last a few seconds and can save your verse or chorus. Did I just say save?

I keep thinking about that scene in the movie *Spinal Tap* where band member David St. Hubbins says, "It's such a fine line between clever and stupid." In your arrangements, it's a fine line between clever and cheesy. Think about it, does your melodic or arrangement idea sound like everyone else? Is it that generic? Is it unique but sticks out as if it doesn't belong in this song? Does it come across as the best part of the song, the most interesting? If so, you have a problem with the basic foundation of the song. The problem might just be the song itself.

Remember a great arrangement never turns a bad song good. This fact you really need to adhere to in writing your arrangement. The arrangement should be the support for the song, the story, and the melody. This way you will never outpace the song. You may have to go back to the song itself and re-write some of it. This is OK, since it's better to find out the weaknesses now than to spend hundreds of hours on a single song and when it's done still wonder why this part of the project just doesn't come across.

Themes

You know those repeating motif's that are so catchy? They're one of the basics of pop music. The motif can be anything, a percussion part, a guitar riff, a keyboard line, and background vocal answer to the lead. Or it could be the melody itself. These elements carry an awful lot of weight when you look at how they are used within your favorite hits. Sometimes you can use the background vocal as the lead melody and in the spaces use lead vocal lines or riffs to accentuate the message. By doing this you shift the emphasis of the story (in a loose kind of way) with the lead vocal and a structured melody with the backgrounds. Guitar or synth themes can be the "glue" that fills and ties the vocal lines together.

There are so many possibilities. It's your creativity that will dictate here. This type of hook is as important as the melody itself. Look to the integral line of the song's chorus as it may give you a hint as to what can be used or what is needed. I wish I could just wave a magic wand and give you directions on how to do it, but this is where your individuality comes in. Having a strong song is a big part of the battle, but complementing that song with strong arrangement elements is just as important.

Part II

Performance of That Song

CHAPTER 2

The Best Drum Parts Are in the Phone Book

Have you ever been to a club on "Guest Star" night and listened to the house band get through their set and you think that the drum sound isn't very good. You may think it's a bad kit, or poorly miked or poorly mixed. Then a guest drummer gets up on stage, same drums, same sticks, same everything. He sits down, clicks off "one, two, three, four" and it all sounds different. The kick is tight and solid, the snare is sharp and full at the same time, the feel is solid and what a great groove. You blink your eyes, because you can't believe it… it's only been a few minutes since the other drummer was on that same kit.

Great players are *great* players, yes they are. I've seen and heard that same scenario I told you about, it seems hundreds of times, but in the studio when it really counts. They come up with absolutely the right part at the right time. It's simply creativity, that brute force that we all want to have all the time. There are only a few who possess this trait all the time. They are the studio pros…

the people who you hear on everyone's albums. From coast to coast, these players travel with their instruments ready and willing to add that special something to your recording.

Wow, pulling this talent together and planting the seed to guide these people to the destination you want is the magic of that communication between musicians, all at the same time. Don't get me wrong, I'm not advocating that all recording be done by the elite few who rule as session musicians, how boring would that be? Moreover, just pick your battles.

You're Not Superman!

Yes, you can play it yourself, but if it takes you three months to get a great guitar part, how long will it take you to complete the whole project... Is the song, the sound, or the arrangement still as viable? Is the record company executive that signed you still in power, now that it's two years later? If you need help on one song... make that call.

If you can do the rhythm part perfectly, but are having a real time of it getting any leads done... get help. If you can't seem to get the feel right on a tune, bring in an extra percussionist that plays along to solidify the feel and tempo. Let your drummer play to a human, not a click track. These are all ways to add that element of total professionalism without pegging your music or your sound within defined limits.

Prioritize the time you spend, especially if there is a deadline. Whether or not you're signed, don't get bogged down in all of the intricacies of the project. Time is not on your side. You're not getting any younger, you might be getting more experience true, but the genre is changing right in front of your eyes and ears. Bottom line; get some help if and where you need it.

Play it together, what a concept. When musicians are in the same room with eye contact, hearing what each other are playing without walls or barriers, the magic seems to happen so much easier. I know that with so many projects done at home, writers working on the song and recording all their ideas as they go along, piecing together a track that can sound great.

That said, as a producer I would like to say how much better or different could it be if the track to your new song was cut by a group of musicians all playing it at the same time. There is a feel when you get great players into a communicative and creative environment. In fact when you get four players into a room even if they all aren't great, the communication and ideas that come out can be amazing.

The Arrangement

BE TRUE TO YOUR GENRE

Being unique is one of the hardest things to do. There is so much music recorded today in every way imaginable that sounds just like everything and everyone else. To be truly unique comes directly from the unique approach to your unique song. You know what you like, right? You know how to get that feel, right? You've had experience with your type of music, right? Then make sure you stay the course and do whatever feels right for you! This can be hard if what you are doing isn't hot on the charts today. This is where you have to state the vision of your sound.

This is where the roadblocks for your art seem to be at every crossing, every record company, and every club. If what you're doing is great, unique, professional, there will be an imaginative creative A&R guy somewhere that will latch on to what you are doing. A guide to success here is to not show any of your new art form until it's really great and professional.

As you start to perceive the arrangement, look to the number one element that needs to be heard for the listener to even get it. What is this element? It could be the chorus melody, could be the feeling that comes out lyrically in the verse, it could be anything, but it's your job to identify it. This is the foundation of your big picture. Now focus on this element and see where it takes you. Does the genre you work in need a simplistic rhythm track to show off the melody? Does the melody need chord support for it to make sense? Does the lyric need to be spiked rhythmically to increase its impact or simplicity? Where are the leading tones within your chord structure, do they move the melody forward? All of these questions will be answered automatically as you gain more and more experience in creative arrangement. Although, in the beginning, there will always be questions that remain unanswered, it really does get easier as you go. Just keep at it. You will find the way that makes your music unique and accessible to the market you are going into.

DO WHAT YOU DO BEST

You must be good at what you like or else you wouldn't think that what you do is good. Be objective, think of what is on the radio, played in clubs, and not only in your neck of the woods… think globally. The world is a big place. Somewhere there is someone who will think your tunes are the best thing since sliced bread.

Somewhere your melody is way too cool. Somewhere your art is ripe and ready.

This is the trick that usually takes a couple of years to figure out. I've always thought that an overnight success was really an 8- to 10-year proposition. That is, six years to perfect your art and another two to four years to learn how to market your art and find the right people. I'll talk more about that later.

KNOW THYSELF, KNOW THY COMPETITION

When I say perfect your art, I really mean make it commercially or competitively viable, where it can do battle with anything on the radio, out today or even out in the future if you're really on it. I know that's hard to realize since the artists that you hear today in your genre have already learned how to achieve their sound and learned how to market their music. This is your competition, and don't forget it. The end customer has $18.00 in his pocket, goes into a record shop, and has a big decision to make. There are 70,000 titles in front of him and more being added every day. Which *one* to buy, that's the big question, and you've got to hope you have the answer. Do you get into record shops and listen on those headphones to music that will soon be your competition? If you don't, go do it. Get into stores and start listening. Knowledge is king here and using this information and data will help you all along the way.

Now, getting back to your arrangement and your sound, look to where the song takes you. You might think there are no new "feels." Well, maybe today everything in your genre might sound similar, but it's your job to come up with that new one. History does show us that just when you think there is nothing new, bang, out comes the next big thing, and it is in the feel of the song's arrangement where the sound starts to be different. If you have an idea of what's cool for your song, go with it and then make little additions, changes, alterations, and such to the feel to solidify your own unique sound. The changes don't need to be great and overwhelming, just subtle and clever. These subtleties are the trendsetters of the future.

KEEP ON TOP OF TRENDS

Knowing what was popular yesterday and knowing what is popular today gives you a timeline to be able to see into the future in the form of educated guesses. Think about how the trend from last year slipped into the trend this year. You should be able to imagine approximately where that trend line may go later this year. You do notice I said, "*May go.*" It's calculated guessing, but you can hedge your bet. The record shop is a great place to do this research. Understand that being on top of the trends will take a bunch of your time and energy.

The history of production can be a great help. To listen and learn how producers, artists, and engineers of yesterday did sounds, arrangement, and instrumentation are all clues to how you should do it today. I'm not saying copy their ideas or arrangements, moreover just listen and learn how they approached their sound and learn to use some of the same focus on your sound.

Now, do you take chances or not? Think about where this product is going. Is it going to a record company A&R department? If so, make your message concise, although make sure it's unique. I was speaking to a couple of friends the other day who are working on a record to release via Internet and their own label. After listening to some of their songs and arrangements I wondered why they were being so cautious.

"Take chances" I told them and gave them a bunch of ideas so their music would not be so predictable. The ideas aren't revolutionary, just a tiny bit risky. What do you have to lose? Why play it so safe? Are you worried that the audience won't like it? Not being cheesy in your arrangement ideas was the point I tried to get across to them. There was one point in their song where the lead singer hit the title word of the song very short and abruptly. They had put a typical timed delay on it, and believe me it was pretty cheesy.

I suggested that they either have the lead singer come in and re-sing the "delays" as if they were yelled, then re-amp it through a small tube amp with a ton of distortion, add that into the original and then put a reverse reverb on it. It would occupy the same amount of space since their arrangement was based around that bar of dead silence. (Except for the ¾-note timed delays.) This was not rocket science, just a focal point. It is the payoff of the chorus. Make sure it's unique. Make sure it pays off to the listener.

The production value of your project, I have one extra word of advice: don't do so much that it camouflages the song. I mean it, be careful. With all the software, plug-ins, tricks, and gizmos around today it's real easy to overdo the production aspect and alter the artistic focus on the song. To enable the song and your sound to co-exist is sometimes a real feat and will take a lot of work to be unique.

Part III

Sound of That Song

CHAPTER 3

Does It Sound Good?

This is the immortal question, "Does it sound good?"

Well, sound good to whom? Does it compete with the sounds you like on radio or on other records? In the opening part of this book I stated, "do not invert the three elements of hit records." What's left is all the subjective stuff that in the end is only the icing on the cake. A great sound never made a hit record, but a hit record with a great sound will be an even bigger hit!

Sound has always been quite personal. It's always been a mystery to me how electronic design engineers can spend hours on test equipment and never listen to what's coming out of a couple of speakers. Listening, using those two things on the sides of our heads. Some of us like our music bass heavy, some of us like it overly bright. It's the difference between night and day, or in other words, to each his own.

In audio, some think if you use a particular piece or brand name of gear, everything that runs through it must sound good. This piece of gear or program is the best and everything else sounds bad. Well, it just isn't so. The quality of the sound that you hear from the speakers is directly attributed to the source. You know, the player. But, this subjective part of music and sound is very different for different people! What one person likes could sound bad for the next person.

There are many rules you can follow when working in a recording environment, some to be adhered to, others to be selectively broken. If you're working on something and it just doesn't sound right or you can't communicate to the other people what it is you have in your head… don't be afraid to ask for help. During my career there were many times other producers, engineers, musicians, or writers would call me up to ask for help, ask me to come over to their home studios, or their production studios, to see if I could solve their dilemma. If they can ask me, there's no reason for you to not ask for help of the people you know. I know I have asked for help hundreds of times.

I'm not going to toot my own horn here, but great producers and engineers really do know their stuff. They can guide you through the maze of ideas, directions, and possibilities with the greatest of ease. You will never know when your producer just planted that seed of creativity in you that will birth a hit song, with a hit arrangement, with a hit sound, and you didn't even work at it… you just played. You just did what comes naturally with just a little push.

These are the best of times when it all comes together without work. There are the other times when you try and try, and never come up with the right thing, but the producer knows when to say "stop" and look back at what worked on the last tune and why it's not working here. This is when the expertise and experience comes into play. Knowing those tricks and cool production ideas is really helpful. Experience will help here, so just go with it.

As a producer you need to guide the session, focus the engineer and keep track of absolutely everything and every idea. This is a daunting task facing you on a daily basis. Take notes! If you can, learn how to notate musically and fast. If you keep a little book on each project you'll be so organized that doing the session will become a creative experience not one of continuous searching. When I said learn notation, someone has to sketch out ideas that come along. There are electronic ways to notate, go get one of those small micro-recorders that uses mini-cassettes or a flash recorder. Always have it on the console, with fresh media, just in case a great line comes along, or an idea exposes itself. In doing this you can get back to the fun part of creativity quickly and have it memorized on tape.

A great engineer can speed up the creative process. Great engineers really are better than someone who just turned on their first microphone. They take the load off the artist and the producer to let them create, and then there are times when an idea regarding the overall sound of a project is the difference of it having a chance of being heard or not. Communication and creative flow are wonderful things.

Getting in the Studio

So here you are getting ready to go into the studio to record, whether it's your first demo or another new album, it doesn't really matter. You're going into the studio. Hooray!

This reminds me of so many acts that I've had show up "ready to record" and so many that weren't ready at all. One day I started to set up the studio for an extremely well-known artist (who shall remain nameless) that was coming in to record. His roady was unloading guitars, keyboards, amps and the like, while I'm pulling patch cables and setting up the room for just about anything that might come along with this solo artist.

All of a sudden, the roady starts to put a circle of white console tape down behind the console dead center in the sweet spot of the room. And then from this spot he started to make a white tape trail down the two steps, out the door, into the sound lock, past the traffic office, out the front door of the building and up the steps of a Winnebago motor home parked in my parking lot.

I looked up at the guy and asked what he was doing. He replied to me by saying, "I guess you've never worked with *Xxx Xxxxx* before have you?" I said, "No, I haven't." Then he said to me, "Well, by the end of any session, *Xxx* can barely find the front door, let alone a hotel room somewhere, so I parked this rented motor home here and he'll be living in it for the next three months."

You know, that wouldn't have been such bad idea if it hadn't been the middle of the summer where the temperature in the parking lot would top out at 105 degrees every day by noon. That poor Winnebago got pretty gamey by the end of the first month (see illustration).

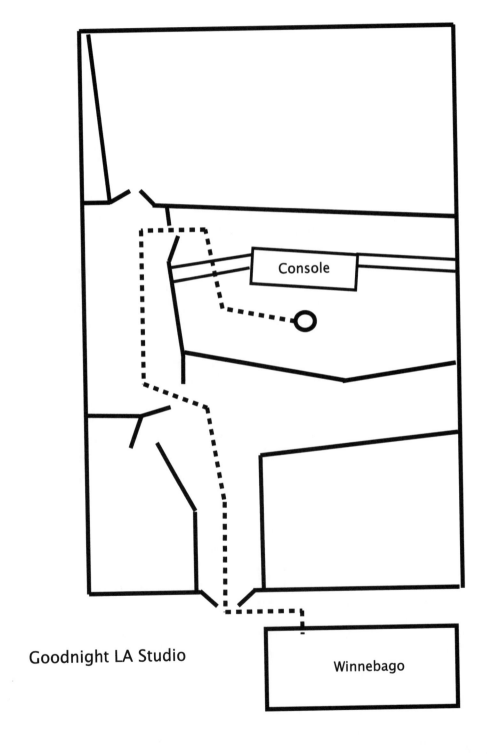

Goodnight LA Studio

Winnebago

Console

I hope you got a chuckle out of that. This just goes to prove that there are no scenarios that you can leave behind. Be primed for anything, because anything is what's going to happen. There are times when your time in the studio will run like clockwork and you'll have a great time creating your music. Then there will be the other times when there is not one thing normal, easy, quick, or fun. Just make the best of it and you'll get to the next day where things may be normal again.

Preparation is critical here; the more time you spend outside of the studio the better you'll be in the studio. I'm not saying that you should rehearse so much that you sterilize the hell out of your material, but just be prepared.

Home Recording

Today there are so many home project studios around that do a very good job of recording and making a product that rivals ones done at larger more expensive facilities. Yes, you can record it at home, although lead vocals might be cheaper and much more efficient in a pro studio. Think of the time and money you'll spend buying cool microphones, high-end preamps, real (not emulated) compressors. Keep in mind your vocal is the most important part of the whole.

What I'm saying here is decide what hat you're wearing. Are you the lead singer, lead guitarist, engineer, or whatever? If you are the artist, the music and performance is much more important than your engineering. To make sure that you're thinking of the performance first, not if the level is right, that's the focus you need to have. If you see my point, then go to a studio where there is someone who can take care of the mechanical aspect of your recording. This could be a friend's home studio, or your home studio with an outside engineer or other band member who has learned enough to get your parts on tape. Just make sure your focus is on the part or hat you have on. Then do the math. Is it cheaper to do it at home, even after buying all the real cool kits to capture your vocal? Or will it be best to record it somewhere else and then edit it at home? You can always pick the best parts from several virtual tracks at home.

Is Building a Home Studio Worth It?

Quick answer: Sure, *if you're already technical*. And believe me, you need to be technical.

So many times I've seen or heard about a band working on writing, practicing, getting tight, starting to play clubs and work, work, working on being great as a band. Then, after getting signed to a marginal record deal, they decide to go down to the music store to buy a bunch of recording gear. They get a great computer, a bunch of software, I/O boxes, a bunch of plugins, preamps, cables, stands, some kind of mixer, outboard gear, racks to house it all, headphones, speakers, media to record on, and all of a sudden they've spent $40,000 of the $50,000 they got from the record company to deliver an album. Oh, and now they have 20 manuals they need to read and study in order to turn on (let alone be proficient with) the gear.

Let me just bring up one phrase: Word Clock. Do you know what it means? Now that you bought all that gear you better know what it means, because not only is the Word Clock ticking, but the record company Delivery Clock is ticking too.

So, to continue on with the scenario, you start reading the first manual, I'll just suggest it's Logic or Pro Tools for instance. Lo and behold, it's three months later, after all the gear is finally hooked up, and you're finally ready to turn on the first microphone.

Think about this; did the record company sign you for your fantastic engineering abilities, or great drum mic placement techniques? No, I think not, you were signed for the art that you can create. That's what is saleable for them. Now, it's still three months later, you've paid yourselves to be in your home studio while you learn how to run all this stuff, you've paid your rent, bought beer, and paid the phone bill. The A&R guy calls and says he's coming over to hear the progress that he bought for $50,000. What do you think is going to happen?

There's no money left, no product, no start on anything. Red flags start waving in front of the A&R guy's eyes. That's when A&R people start calling record producers and studio owners asking them to take a band into the studio for big points and a bunch of recently purchased used gear. My suggestion to you if you're not technical is to use a friend's home studio or someone's project studio and pay him a bit for the favor.

Jumping into Pro Tools has a two year or so learning curve. And besides, getting good at Pro Tools is not good enough; you need to be great at using it. Remember that producer or engineer that may get your gear as that clock continues ticking? Make a deal with them in front. Get help from the engineer to set up the studio, get started making music, cutting basic tracks, doing the foundation of your music. It's like the oil filter commercial; pay me a little now or pay me a lot later. *Get help* and remember the music, it comes first!

Hooked on the Gear and Not the Hook

What is the best gear to use, you ask? I can't say because each and every project is a bit different and as time moves on, the gear changes. What's good for some producer or engineer in a magazine advertisement is not necessarily the best for you. You are the technical creative force behind your music, and that's part of this art too, so don't forget.

You look through the music magazines and you're assaulted by the huge amount of gear positioned to be the best for this, the best for that. Well, maybe your music is different (and I hope it is). Do you want to record your album on your e-mail box in your den? Do you buy a mission specific box, load in a bunch of native software programs to record, or do you do it with some embedded hardware? All are viable ways to record at home.

However, this is your chance at the gold ring. Do not compromise your chances. That said, look to what works within your budget—zeros and ones all sound basically alike. Where are the quality aspects of your art vulnerable? The cheapest mode of recording is not necessarily the best way in the long run. So where do you scrimp and scrape to just enable yourself to get started? Whatever you do, don't scrimp on the origin of sounds. That is, a few really good microphones, a good preamp or two, great instruments and especially a good pair of speakers to listen to what you are getting. You must have an accurate picture.

I remember this one instance where a writer worked on a song for weeks, totally perfected it, called me over to hear it, and when I got there the file wouldn't open… it was corrupted, lost forever… The writer was totally bummed; he says to me "one of my best songs, lost for-ever." Well the happy ending of this story was that he remembered most of it and ended up rewriting some of the lyrics anyway.

Please don't let this happen to you. We've already lost so much of the music of a generation to ADAT and DA-88 tapes, early computer files, and DAT cassettes that will not play anymore. Back up your songs on several different media formats. Don't just do it as files on hard disks, but also do it as PCM on CDR or DVD-R, or as individual tracks on 2" analog. Let's give the record company a chance to recoup what they've given to us as up front money so we could record in the first place.

Building your own studio can be the happiest day of your life, but later down the road it could also be your worst mistake. Choose wisely what gear you like and buy. Start a relationship with a store that sells the gear you think you'll need; there is usually someone at the music store that knows what they are talking about. Read up on how other artists in your genre recorded their album; see if you can find out how much help they had in the beginning.

All of the gear in the world won't bring out any tal-ent; they are just tools, your palette, your paintbrush, and your pen and in the worst case will zap your creative drive. What I mean by that is if there is no deadline, no real reason to finish today, no reason to drive you that little bit harder to finish a project and deliver it, human nature will put off till tomorrow what should be done today.

Where to start? Pick the mode or way you want to record. If you pick a native solution you will now enter the realm of the "anything is possible" scenario. Now decide whether or not you're going to be the technical wizard as well. It will be a hard decision since so much of today's music is entrenched in technology and a simple rhythmic groove.

The time you take up front in this decision process will be the best time spent. Know what you're getting into. So be careful on what you choose to record on... sooner or later you will have to deliver it hopefully to a label for distribution. You will have to deliver all the tracks, elements, EDL, etc. on a format that can be opened a decade from now when there is no such thing as a G5 (they have been lost to the junk heap five years earlier), "my God we're on G8's now." All those IDE or SCSI drives, FireWire schmire-wire (now say it's year 2014) are relics of a bygone era in computing.

These are issues that record companies have been facing for generations. What delivery format will be around for 50 years? So far, the only one that has stood the real test of time is analog tape. Hard disc manufacturers actually state that drives are reliable for 3 years, if and only if, they are spun up at least once every 90 days. This is the mean time before first failure. Now you know! *Back up* again and again. Remember those drives on your shelf hold all your songs, all that creativity... Back them up to every format you have, CDR, DVD, or any and all other drives.

On the companion web site for this book (http://www.courseptr.com/downloads) are links to resources to help you archive your own works, deliver product to a record company, and learn basic necessities of track organization. Use them, download them, print them out and keep with all of your hard drives and data discs.

CHAPTER 4

The Recording Process

You're Responsible for the Vibe

Your job as the producer is to guide the creativity, even if it's only you. That last statement is pretty all encompassing isn't it? When there are too many chiefs, the project can, and will, become out of focus. There always needs to be a leader, but wearing a particular hat and defining everyone's role is very important and incredibly tenuous. We *play* music, not work at it, right? First of all, make sure that this experience is fun.

I remember one project that I was involved with where I co-produced an act with a very creative guitarist/writer/singer. We started out on this project knowing that it would take a couple of months, but as the project dragged on past the eight weeks, we knew that we had to buckle down and work some long hours and get it done. As we finished the last mix, my co-producer said to me that he would be unavailable for at least a week, so don't even bother calling him. A week later he called me to see how the mastering went and when I asked him where he was, he told me he took an amp, his guitar, drove off, and just played for seven days straight. He said to me that he had forgotten the reason he got into this business. It was for the music and the pleasure of just playing his guitar. This is the true reason we need to remember that we go and "play" in the studio, perform in the studio, and for God's sake have a great time making music.

Remember *play* is that four-letter word. It's your job to make sure you're having a good time. Making music is fun and a privilege not to be taken so seriously that the "vibe" will bring down a session. The feeling you get when you cut a great track, you feel so good, your ego is pumped up, and it's magnificent. Now to keep this under control is a neat trick, there is a deadline, a budget, a group of very creative people that all need the same attention. It's all about "bedside manner," that comfort you give to each individual, each member of the band, which allows them to expose themselves in front of a microphone.

As an artist producing yourself, there are even more pressures that get put directly on you. Not only are you responsible for the art, the song selection, the sound, guiding the other musicians, working with the engineer, communicating with the label, and on and on. Now with all this pressure you still have the responsibility to capture your art in a way that is accessible to your audience. This can seem like an impossible task. You may be right, although if you do your homework up front plus choose your allies and other creative forces you plan to use carefully, this can be a very pleasing experience, one where you're in control of all aspects of your destiny.

On to the Studio

Now with some of the possible scenarios laid out, let's look to the process of recording from the technical beginning. Oh good, here come the drawings. Try out these remedies I've put together to get you started. They will keep you out of trouble at first. Later on, when there's no pressure, start doing it your way. There is no absolute correct or incorrect way of doing just about anything in the studio.

Microphones and Placement

I would always say to myself three simple words to keep a recording on track, which are "Remember the Source."

If you always look to the source of the sound and make it sound as good as possible at the origin, then the microphone technique you use will be much less important and the engineering skills you possess will not be as critical. Think about all the ways the human ear perceives sound, how the ear differentiates between wanted and unwanted sound. The microphone can't do this, period. It hears what is in its pattern and what is within its specifications.

In this section I will name a few of the usual suspects when it comes to individual microphones, but in general what you have will probably be OK. It's much more important to have a great part played well than a poor part not played very well, and a great mic.

I'll give you some placement ideas for these, but always use your own ears. Trust your ears explicitly. You're there. I'm not. Destructive interference will be mentioned several times in the following pages whenever

35

there is more than one mic on a single sound source. Be careful, take your time, learn the basics, and from your experience you'll have an understanding of where to go first. Look at the drawings and see where the problem areas are, where you can get into trouble, and how to stay out of it.

DRUMS

Most recordings have some form of drum tracks... if you're starting with a kit of drums look to the following pages to give yourself a head start on getting a sound that is close to the sound of the instrument itself.

Have I talked about phase yet? At first try to set up all your mics on the same plane, so to speak... just follow the arrows... this way the phase correlation will at least be at 0 degrees. Then any phase anomalies will be time related not because you've placed some mics 90 degrees or so out of phase with another one.

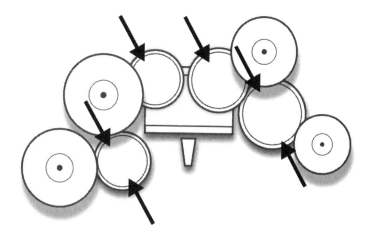

Kick Drum

Lets start with a kick drum, it being one of the essentials of most recordings. What do you want to hear from it? If there is a hole in the front head and there is some damping inside, do you mic it from the inside as well? Let's go through the particulars one at a time:

Does the beater have a hard or soft head on it? This will determine the amount of high frequency output of the spike. If the head has a beater strike pad this will give "thud" along with the spike. If you mic from the inside, make sure that the phase relationship is inline with the snare drum mic. We'll cover that in detail later on.

Do you want after-sustain or the actual ambience of the drum as a resonance of head itself? To get this the best way is to use a DW resonator placed in front of the kick. They work great. If you don't have access to a resonator you may want to use two mics on the kick, one up by the beater and one outside the front head, but away from the hole. Be careful with the tuning of this front head, don't get it too tight, just let it flap in the wind, but with a bit of after ring.

A little hint here is to have a bit of spray lubricant handy to eliminate any squeaks in the pedal mechanism that always seems to be heard at the end of tunes. The kick and the snare will be the two loudest percussion elements within your recording, so spend a bit of extra time making sure they sound the way you want.

Now let's examine that phase relationship stuff. Try to place the snare mic and the kick mic with their capsules in the same direction. What each mic hears will give a positive pulse at the input of the console upon impact. Make sure that these two mics are in phase with each other! Spend time on this. You will be happy with the outcome.

Snare Drum

I've always found that an SM57 works great and can take a beating. Yes, they do get hit from time to time. The mic angle to the drum's head, which makes up part of that phase relationship to the angle of the kick drum mic (and every other mic on the kit), is very important here. Once again I stress, try to keep it on the same plane. I say this because the kick and snare usually end up dead center in your mix, so any phase anomalies reflect themselves as nodes in the frequency response.

A lot of engineers use top and bottom mic placements to be able to capture more of the snare wire itself. To do this, note the angle that you placed the top mic, then at the exact opposite, place the lower mic. Then make sure you electronically reverse the phase 180 degrees. Be careful with how much of this mic you use, since the sound will always be pretty raspy at best.

Toms

You know there are simple rules to follow when close miking a set of toms. The rule of thumb is keep as many of the mics on the same phase relationship as the snare as possible. I've used so many different mics here, but lately I've been using the clip-on Audio Technica ATM 35's since they are so small and easily placed. Talk about easy, the clip holds the mic very well and the mini gooseneck allows you to position the mic anywhere you want.

Top and bottom mic techniques can be used if you have enough inputs on your console. The bottom mic seeks out the rumble and pitch of the toms, while the top mic hears the attack. Remember the tuning of both heads is very important.

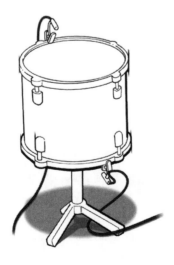

A simple guide here is to keep the top and bottom mics at 180 degrees from each other and flip the phase.

Also angle the floor toms a bit so that the stage or floor they're on doesn't create a standing wave. That mic doesn't know the difference between the initial attack and the reflected wave coming directly up off the floor. Angle of incidence equals angle of reflection.

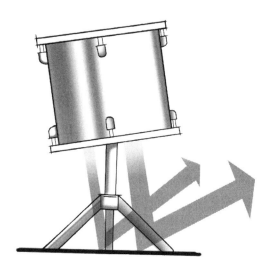

Overhead & Cymbals

The trick here is to get the mic high enough to not get the splash as the cymbals move, but to get an overall sonic image of the kit. Don't place them too high or the mics will hear the reflections off the ceiling that could be destructive. I use a quality condenser mic here with a good cardioid pattern. Look to phase correlation here again.

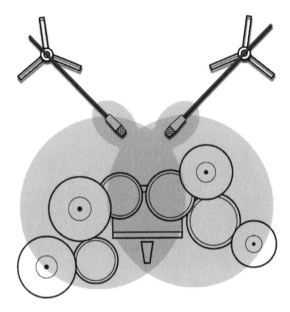

You can do an XY pattern as shown in the illustration or just have them hear the cymbals by placing the mics close to the left and right crashes. Use your ears and note that each drummer's setup can be very different.

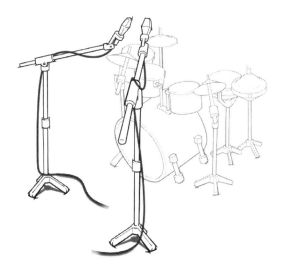

Hi-Hat

Especially here, look to phase correlation to the snare drum as these two elements are very close together. You can use most anything on the hat, but if you use a dynamic, make sure you turn off the phantom power to not increase distortion. Have I emphasized phase enough yet?

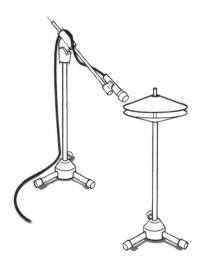

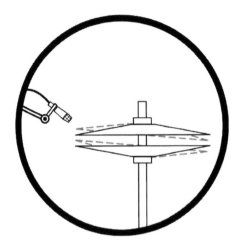

AMBIENCE MICS

This is where you can be very clever with the room sound of the kit as a whole or by gating these mics, keyed from a sum of the toms, you can get a more "Phil Collins" sound. Don't get them too far away from the original sound source or you will not get ambience, you'll get delay!

Delay is probably not what you're looking for. Remember, if the human ear can perceive delays starting at 15ms, do the math (a millisecond equals about 13 inches) and find out where in the room you hear the most reflections on the kit. Make sure you're less than 15 feet from the original source. This distance is just a guide. Rules are made to be broken.

ACOUSTIC GUITARS

On an acoustic guitar, there is a complex placement procedure. The best thing here is to use your ears. Get out on the studio floor and listen. Move around until you hear what you think the mic will hear. Place it right there. I've used small capsule condensers about 3 to 5 inches away for the guitar halfway between the hole and the heel of the neck, just about at the 14th fret. Every occasion will be different, somewhere between that 14th and 19th fret is a good place to start, use your best gear and ears for this. Multi-mic techniques are good too.

ELECTRIC GUITARS

Here is where the amp is king. If you make the amp sound good with the settings and the physical guitar plugged into it, you're more than halfway home. Where to place the amp in a room? Where to place the mic on the amp? Open air or corner?

I would suggest putting the amp in a corner off the floor about 18 inches. Even if the amp has a closed back you still get the corner loading, so you pick up some low bottom end. Then turn the amp all the way up so you hear hiss coming out of the amp. Put on some head-phones fed from the control room of say a SM57 you have in your hand. Move the mic around and listen until the mic picks up the highest pitched hiss. You'll find this spot is usually directly over the edge of the voice coil out about 1 inch from the grill cloth. This is the sweet spot for the most average crunch sound. Mark this spot on the grill with a bit of china marker.

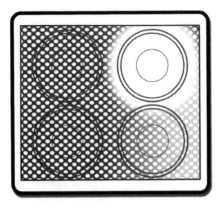

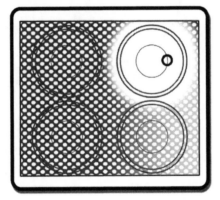

Now why do I say place the speaker cabinet at least 12 to 18 inches above the floor? Look at the angles if you distance mic the amp at all... say even a few feet the ratio between direct and reflected sound... the greater the angle the better off you are. *Wow,* Leo Fender had the right idea on those old twins and super reverbs with the two legs on the sides of the amp to angle it back. They sounded so clear and rich to a mic.

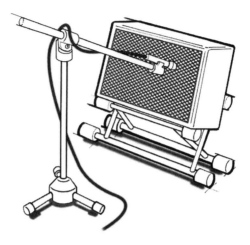

When it comes to that ratio of direct to reflected sound think about the ceiling too; as you aim the amp upward you're actually filling the room with sound not just aiming it at the nearest wall. This is all about diffusion, especially if you're looking to add an ambience mic into the mix. As you aim it upwards the first reflection is a long way away, and by the time it gets back to the mic it's been reflected off several walls, the floor, and on and on.

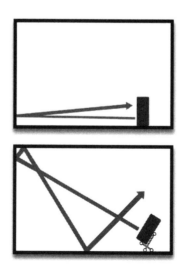

The other area where you could run into problems is the guitar cable itself. With guitar cords it is simply the shorter the better. The guitar cord is just a capacitor across the signal from hot to ground. The longer the cable the more capacitance there is, the less top end you have. Low capacity special cables are great, but don't look to them for a whole lot of difference since the source impedance of the guitar is pretty high and the input impedance of most amps is high. The rule again is: the shorter the cord, the better the sound. If you have to remote locate the speaker cabinet (say in a different room), use *big* speaker cable between the head and speakers. Don't scrimp here, the output transformer and output tubes won't like it.

The word to the wise is *experiment*. There are guidelines and rules of thumb, and there will always be another way to do it. Ways like multiple mics, multiple speaker cabinets, non-matched speakers, and dual heads to dual cabinets, electronic crossovers to separate heads, then separate speakers in separate rooms. There will always be another way to do it.

BASS

A good direct box is essential, preferably a good transformer DI. They are so warm that the bass will actually sound like a bass. Using an amp is also necessary to get that push of air within the initial attack. Compression is necessary because the bass occupies so much real estate within your mix, it's good to keep it even.

When you put a mic on the amp, once again, use your ears along with your brain. What do you want out of the amp? Is it the overtone structure? Is it the crunch and overload? Or is it just a bit of believability that it's a real bass and not just a synthesizer?

Here is where you mic it accordingly. If you just need that air from a speaker trying to reproduce bottom end transients, then corner load the cabinet and mic close to the outer support web of the speaker. If you need the overtones, mic directly inline with the edge of the voice coil. If you desire that crunch, adjust the amp controls until you hear the sound you want then mic for what the amp is doing, maybe a foot or so away.

PIANOS

Please use your ears. It really is the only way to find the best placement for the mics. You can use any number of directional condenser mics for this purpose. You may want to use two mics to separate the "left hand" and the "right hand" this is not totally true, as far as separation, although you are capturing a great stereo image. A bit of compression is helpful here if there's not too much ambient leakage from other instruments. In the beginning, mic the circles below.

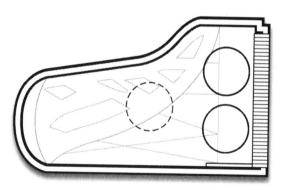

LESLIES ON ANYTHING

A Leslie is a stereo device that can be very grand indeed. The spinning of the top horn creates that wonderful

Doppler effect we've grown to know and love. The bottom, rotating drum will give the rest of the pulse of the Leslie. I always loved the way the top rotor and the bottom drum slowed down differently.

To mic a "normal" Leslie cabinet, take two mics on the top and one on the bottom. Be prepared to use two tracks for this stereo effect. The top mics are placed at 180 degrees of each other and the bottom mic is placed near the bottom rotor. Use a windscreen on all mics. Try a couple of Shure SM57's on the top and something that has good bottom response on the lower rotor.

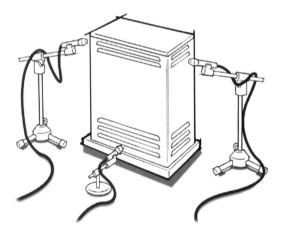

A Fender guitar Leslie is a full range device that rotates like a wheel of a car. Here, place two mics 180 degrees to each other on the sides and record them to two tracks. Here again watch out for wind pops when it's on the fast position.

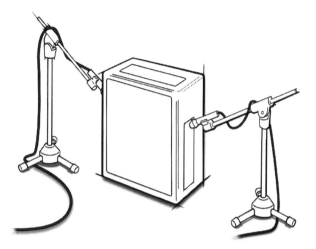

Here you must not be too close with the mics since there are escape holes for the rotating drum on three sides. So if you mic it on the left and right sides and not the top you have a more definite stereo shift left to right, and a bit of a dip when the rotor is either straight up or straight down. This can be a good thing.

VOCAL MIC

The lead vocal mic technique has a couple of schools of thought. First there is the close mic technique where there is the proximity effect of bottom end build-up. To accomplish this you must use a windscreen or every P or B and even some T's and some C's will pop and distort. It is a way of securing a very intimate vocal sound. Use a great mic and you'll always be happy. If the proximity effect is too much, move the windscreen away from the mic or even put up a dummy mic and place the actual mic you're using either above and a bit behind the dummy.

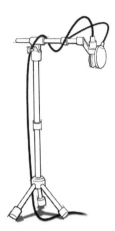

The other method is the distant mic technique of placing the mic above the vocalist and just letting them sing. This is sometimes hard for the artist who wants to give a performance singing into thin air, but the sound, especially for female vocalists, is second to none. Just make sure that your singer doesn't try to sing "up" into the mic; this could cause them to stretch and injure their larynx. This is the lead vocal, the single most important part of any recording, so you must treat it with respect.

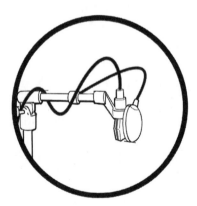

Try things like double compression, sending to delayed chambers pre-compression, putting high frequency expanders on the vocal, etc. All are ways to add life and intelligibility to the vocal. See the high frequency expander block diagram.

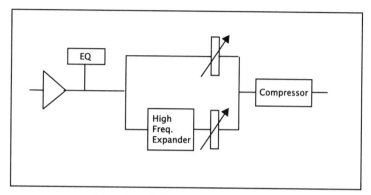

Vocal High Frequency Expander

Foldback

Headphone mixes are probably the most important part of the recording process. It is the way the artist hears his performance against the rest of the instruments. There are two schools of thought in recent years: (1) give the artist a great sounding mix from inside the control room, and (2) give the artist an infinite amount of choices and let them blend it any way they want with an individual mixer at every player. This is an area where you shouldn't skimp. Quality at any cost is what I always preach.

Pitch Reference

Let's talk about foldback pitch reference or the combination of tones that a vocalist will hear and reference their own pitch consciousness around. There lies the main reason why I don't like the individual mixers for each artist. It just isn't consistently repeatable. What if the lead vocal has a problem that doesn't rear its ugly head until weeks later in the project? Will the singer be able to adjust this individual mixer to the exact same mix as he had weeks earlier? The chances are slim to none.

Sometimes this won't be a problem, but when it is, you may have entered into a pitching hell you wish you had control over.

For those of you who have the luxury of using a digital console, all I can say is keep memorizing (saving) a separate mix as you go along. This is the best way to keep a file of the lead vocal headphone mix, the tracking headphone mix, the background vocal headphone mix, etc. This way you have the headphone mix, the mic setup, the effects balance, and on and on. If you have a simple analog mixer, then use your best judgment and try to always print or record your balance of all the instruments to a couple of tracks. By doing this you have essentially memorized the pitch reference that you're sending out to the headphones. While you're overdubbing listen only to this two-track mix and the new stuff you're adding.

You're now being smart with your own pitch reference and can help pitch the vocalist by just increasing or decreasing the amount of foldback you give. There will be more on pitch referencing of lead vocals later.

Monitor Mix

Did I emphasize the monitor mix v. headphone mix enough yet? Make sure you're listening to the same mix that you're sending to the studio floor. Why? Well if you're going to be able to help guide the artist with areas of pitch reference, melodic content against the tonality of the track, with conflicting or nonconflicting phrasing against the track, you need to have the same reference to the song, the performance, and the sound as the artist on the floor. If you are listening to the same thing when they ask for more of this and less of that, you can decide where and how much you should adjust and still keep a good solid reference to pitch and rhythm, real or implied.

THE CONSOLE

I'm going to get a bit technical here, so bear with me and try to use common sense where you don't totally understand. When I talk about console gain structure, it's a little like plumbing. Turn on the cold water a little and you get a little out, put a high-pressure pump on the same water and the volume of water increases. Mixing is when you take a little cold water, a little hot water; mix them together until you get a water temperature that is "just right." Now do you want to treat the water, divide out the water to more faucets? A recording mixer or console is pretty much the same sort of idea. I hope you'll understand the next few pages, since if you're recording at home or in your own studio, be aware of the pitfalls of distortion, clipping, or just poor recording.

GAIN STRUCTURE

With every console, even the smallest six-channel analog mixer, how you use the gain of each stage is directly proportional to the output quality.

BEFORE AND AFTER THE MIC PREAMP

Say for instance you have a lot of input level (about a -10db average); you set the gain of this first stage mic preamp at medium (about +20db) and you push the fader up to "0." What's happening to the transients? Now you add +5db at 1500 Hz and wonder why it sounds a bit clipped or just a bit scratchy.

On a larger console there are more than just 3 or 4 gain stages—there could be as many as 20 or even more. The way you set up the gain of the first element is critical to the overall quality. Say you have a condenser mic placed on a Marshall 4x12 cabinet and the head is set for full power. The level at the speaker is nearing 132 SPL, you put the gain of the mic preamp as low as it will go—say about only 10dB of gain you put the fader up to 0 and it sounds flat and clipped? Why? Where is the overmodulation?

Just think of what the mic is doing. This poor element is a few inches away from a very loud sound source. Do you think the mic itself could be clipping? Probably. Go out to the floor and if the mic has an input pad you can select, make sure you use it or change mics to a much lower output device (dynamic mic versus condenser).

Now this example is just brute force of a high output mic on a loud sound source, but what if that same mic is used on an instrument where the transient characteristics are most of the sound as with a snare drum or tambourine? Mic clipping can ruin your sound before the signal ever gets to the console. Knowing what the output is of different signal sources will be one way you can avoid these problems. Think about what components are present. Is it strident with very short duration, as with a wood block with very little after resonance, or is it more RMS signal content, as with a very loud distorted guitar amp? They are both just as loud to the mic for a fraction of a second.

So what to do, you ask? Know the output or sensitivity of your microphones. Choose wisely and get on to the next problem area, the console mic preamp. This high gain device is designed to accommodate a wide variety of signal levels, have adjustable gain control, and sound acceptable at most all gain settings. Good luck! Most preamps do sound very good at a gain window of 20 to 40 db. Now when you ask this preamp to only be an isolation and balanced input device and have no gain is just as bad as when you ask the same amp to give you 80 db of gain.

That gain control device is in the feedback loop of the amplifier; simply stated the more gain you give an amp the greater (less feedback) the distortion of the amp itself. Even more simply said the more feedback you have around an amplifier the less gain you have, and lower the distortion, although to make the circuit so variable the original designers had to compromise with compensation components in the rest of the circuitry and that will influence the sound.

With all this ho-haw, I hope you understand that most everything is compromise of one thing or another. I'm saying the designers had to use elements of electronics that can change the sound. Use a resistive input pad where necessary, then you can increase the gain of the preamp. This puts the preamp in the console into its sweet spot. As you use your mixer more and more you will find where this sweet spot is and where the mic preamp sounds best.

EQ AMPLIFIER

The next gain stage is probably the equalizer. Remember this is a frequency selectable gain device or simply said, some form of a tone control. So if you're adjusting the frequency at or near the fundamental frequency of the sound, you're really mostly adjusting the overall gain.

If you have set the gain of the mic pre to give you about "0" output level and you're using a desk that will overload and distort at +18, when you add a whole bunch of EQ at a particular frequency—say 1500Hz—you may be taking the amp into clipping. All you wanted was a sound you heard in your head, and now you have something completely different. Think ahead of your EQ tastes and understand the fundamental frequencies of instruments, vocals or other sounds. To better understand this, use the Musical Frequency Chart in Appendix B. It really does help.

THE COMBINING OR SUMMING AMP

The next gain stage is the combining amp; this is an isolation amplifier designed to have very low source impedance, near zero if possible. This way the summing resistors will have the highest amount of channel-to-channel isolation. Simply said, when you combine two or more signals together via a resistive bridge (or bunch of resistors tied together to mix the signals together) the isolation is directly proportional to the source impedance.

OK, not so simply said. Remember the plumbing? It's like having hot water in your toilet; I'm sure some of you have heard of that happening.

Now if you have drums, bass, two guitars, vocals, solos, and keyboards all going to the two-track combining buss, what do you think that the little summing amp will sound like if the master fader after this amp is brought down too far just to keep the meter needles from bending? This stage of gain is one of the most suspect when you're mixing. I know it's easier to just bring down the master a bit than to lower all the other faders. My suggestion to you is to start with the master fader all the way up and don't worry about it if the level seems a bit low at first, rest assured it will get higher as you add other tracks.

IT'S ALL ABOUT HEADROOM

Give yourself some headroom. Keep on top of the console and you will stay out of trouble. There are gain stages you can adjust and many that are isolation only and you can't adjust them. The only way is to not hit them so hard in front. Look to the signal path drawings that most mixers have in their manuals. This will give you a pretty good idea of what's ahead and what's behind all that crackling, clipping, and distortion that you're hearing. If you don't understand these signal flow diagrams ask a friend that has a studio or ask an engineer that you know to take a peek at it for you and explain what's going on under the knobs. Remember before when I said *get help*—it can't be truer here.

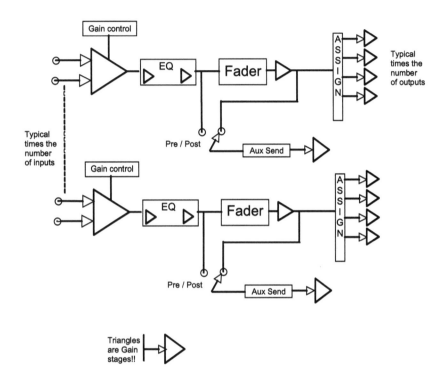

DIGITAL CONVERTERS

If you record digitally, as you get in and out of the console, there will be these boxes that you'll have to deal with sooner or later. It's the digital converter. All of the tech stuff that goes on inside is a miracle to most of us. The sampling rate, the bit depth, the way the actual conversion from analog to digital bits and back works is magic. There are several boxes on the market that do a very good job. There are the brands that sell a lot of units, like the MOTU units, and so many others that are either $100 cheaper or several thousand dollars more expensive.

The reference here is to look at the converter chip used inside. There are really only five or so manufacturers of these chips that are commonly used in the gear that we buy. These are Analog Devices, Crystal by Cirrus Logic, TI, Motorola, and AKM. You know by now, the quality of just about any brand is very good. The new models especially, the way they work and the way they sound is nearly imperceptible. Most of the difference in the sound is dependent on the sample rate, the higher the better for the filter on the D to A to work best. That said, 99% of all product sold to consumers is at a sample rate of 44.1 KHz or less and sometimes compressed to high heaven as with MP3's. Any way you look at it, your product will run through several sets of converters, and half of the time, you'll have no control over the quality of the device located in the home of the consumer.

BIT DEPTH

Just think of the higher the bit depth, the better the sound, the better the dynamic range, and the better the noise specification. Most digital desks have a bit depth internally of at least 24 bit. They are usually 32 bit, and are now 32-bit floating point. This means that you can have internal dynamic range nearing an astronomical 1500 dB. That should do it if you think of the gain structure that you're emulating within an analog desk. The amount of headroom available should enable these new generation of digital desks to rival the sound we're used to hearing in the analog desks of the past. Just think how good a digital desk can sound at 96 kHz/32 bit floating point! On a digital desk that has 24-bit internal processing you can and will run out of headroom, so keep that in mind. As you get into the newer desks you'll find that the firmware writers had a delicate balance between headroom and noise floor. You should have no overloading problems with these newer generations of desks.

CHAPTER 5

Effects

This next section is devoted to processors. Just when you think that you have a handle on what you need and want to use, another manufacturer or software company comes out with something new that someone in a magazine review is swearing that without it you're doomed. I must say remember, "Less is more" when it comes to effects. They can clutter a mix, refocus the intent of the arrangement, or be more predominant than the song itself. If I never hear another vocal run through a "pitch corrector" it will be too soon, especially when the base correction percentage is too high. Use these processors sparingly; they can mask not accentuate the performance or song.

Equalization

Yes, this too is an effect and probably the most widely used one at that. Whenever you start to equalize you're messing with the overtone and harmonic structure of a sound or instrument. I've seen time and time again early engineers start adding 3K to just about everything, with quotes like "everything sounds better with a little EQ on it" coming to mind. This is definitely not true. Everything doesn't sound better with a little or a lot of EQ on it. Say for instance, if the guitar amp is set up correctly, controls adjusted to give the sound you want, and then the right mic placed in the right area, you will have a sound that when you add EQ, it sounds worse. This is a good test of your mic and EQ technique. Remember the source!

Now there are times when you need a lot of EQ, like when layering in drums. The kick seems to sound so much better when you pull out 6 or so db of 410 Hz or so. This is not a trick that should be copied—just use your ears. When the kick has less energy in the 4th through 6th harmonic you can use a bit more chunk of the guitars, and still perceive the kick at the same energy level. It's all about spectrum, but more about that later.

The only hint I can really give is to use your ears not your eyes when equalizing. Keep in mind the fact that you could be overloading the stage of the desk if you bring the signal in at 0 db and add 15 db of mid-bottom end, (at the fundamental frequency). Then you'll wonder why it sounds funky wherever there is a transient attack. See how you ran the desk right out of headroom? If the average input level in VU is 0, then the peak value is usually higher and in some cases a lot higher, depending on which instrument it is, then adding a bunch of EQ at a particular frequency could easily take the channel into clipping.

Don't be afraid of "Air." That is, using very high frequency EQ points, like at 16 kHz or even higher on some analogue desks. This is usually not heard, just perceived. Listen to Mariah Carey's vocals. Think they've used some high top here? Lastly keep a record of what you're doing so when you hit on something great you can come back to it later or even on another song or project.

I remember when a president of a record company once asked me to make sure I called him before I started my first mix on a project for his label. I called and he told me, I quote, "Here at *XYZ* label, we use lots of bottom, lots of middle, and lots of top. So when the mix is done, call me and play the first mix for me over the phone. If you do as I say we've got hits here." Well I gave them what they wanted: lots of bottom, lots of middle, and a whole lot of top.

Compression, Gates, and Other Gain Control Devices

Limiters, compressors, expanders, and gates are all forms of automatic gain control. The compressor is a ratio adjustable gain control device where if you have a 3:1 ratio set up then for every 3 db above the threshold the output raises 1 db. Now you can see how a 20:1 can really clamp down the signal. It's the same as turning up the input to 20 and having the amp only put out 1, but it all happens very quickly triggered by the intensity or level of the incoming signal. Limiters are just 100:1 compressors that are usually used in addition to compressors as an absolute peak limit or ceiling where no signal or transient will exceed. Limiters can take the life out of a performance if there isn't a compressor ahead of it so you can control how this automatic gain control squeezes the sound.

Expanders work in reverse and are useful when the dynamic range of a signal especially on the low side is indistinguishable. Ratios like 1:10 are pretty intense, but ratios like 1:3 can be useful in conjunction with a good compressor. Work with the varied threshold points to bring the dynamic range within reason, both the bottom end of the range along with the top end of the range.

Gates are very quick variable on/off switches, and provide a way of getting rid of the snare drum in the tom mics for example. But there are a million uses: getting rid of the hum on guitar amps, lowering breaths of a lead singer. It's how you use the range control that is the beauty of these devices.

One thing I will talk about here is that on a kit of drums if you use gates on each mic, say where the gate opens to 100% on each tom hit, the toms will then have the overtone of the cymbals included with the sound. The same with the snare, if the gate opens to 100%, the hi-hat will be part of the snare sound. If you're planning on using samples later on to really isolate each drum, make your samples early on using the same kit. This will give you a leg up and keep your own unique sound on the entire kit.

More gate usages for instance, on a lead vocal where the breaths are just too much, put a gate on it first before any compression. Then, adjust the threshold to be just above the level of the breaths. Finally adjust the range to say lower this "off" function by 3 to 6 db, then put a bit of a fast attack and slow release on the gate to smooth out the whole thing.

On most all automatic-gain control devices there is a release time control. Take care and think of the signal you're putting into the device. If the release time is faster than the waveform itself you will cause distortion. Be careful, start with it slow and then speed it up until you have the desired effect.

Reverb: Analog and Digital

Where do I start? Let's see, the best reverbs are chambers made out of brick and mortar, maybe. Well, not really. As in all effects they are input source signal dependent. This is a very important fact. I've heard big perfectly tuned old EMT plates that sound fabulous on vocals and terrible on drums; this is a fact of life, and experience will guide you to which reverb processor is best on which instrument.

Some of the newest digital processors and plug-ins are very, very good. They do so much more than the algorithms of just a few years ago. The Sony and Yamaha pieces are great. The Lexicon 960 or 480L are necessary pieces of gear for most studios. Look at the complement of options you can get your hands on, listen to them outside of your mix, maybe using a CD as program material and get familiar with the characteristics of each unit. Then look inside the various settings and algorithms.

As you try to disseminate all the parameter selections you can modify, just understand that this *will* drive you crazy. Take a little time and read the manual—it will help. Then set up some user banks for you to quickly get to sounds and reverbs that are familiar and will work most of the time. There are no hard and fast rules again, just try to use reverb where it helps and doesn't just smear the performance. Also, one last hint; try to bifurcate or separate the signal from the reverb. OK that's a complicated way of saying use pre-delay to separate the dry signal from any reverb. This way you can use less of the reverb and still have the desired effect of ambience and increased duration and density.

Digital Effects

Delays, chorus/flangers, pitch shifters, auto tuners, high frequency expanders, aural exciters, and more are just the start of the digital effect domain available today at very realistic prices. Most home studios have several "boxes" that can do just about anything. Also, so many plug-ins are available for computer based recording programs. The range is endless. These effects can help and hinder you in the studio. If you arrange a track around a particular delay you're locked into that sound. Sometimes this is great and should be done if you like it. Just remember to record that effect so that it will always be there and not just call it up within a memory bank if you are using outboard gear. What if that piece of gear breaks? Oh great, now you're in for the hell of trying to duplicate that effect on another piece of gear, and it's never quite as good.

DELAYS

Tape delays have been around for years. Remember the Echoplex? In the beginning of Rock n' Roll, technology kept changing how we record and this was one of the first external boxes to really start something big.

The original Gibson Echoplex used a loop of tape where the record head was fixed in one place and the playback head was on a movable slide. As you slid the playback head farther away from the record head the longer the delay. Then there were the feedback controls to allow repeats. As digital effects and vari-speeds on ¼-in tape machines were found in every studio, the Echoplex lived on. When you can, try out one of these "old" devices; you'll be amazed at how good and "real" they sound.

The digital delay has become one of the handiest pieces of gear around. The timed slaps, either quarter note or an eighth note slap, are so handy when you're filling out guitar parts or solos. To find the delay time there are several audio calculating programs (freeware) available on the web.

It's always good to have a stopwatch around the studio to time sections of a tune or calculate the *Beats per Minute* so you can look up your delay times in these programs. Count the beat for 15 sec, multiply by 4, and you're very close. Delays can be used so many ways within other effects to generate different phase correlations from left to right... when the listener is in the center and there is a delay to the right check out what it does to the stereo. Use your imagination.

Automatic Double Track or ADT is when you take a couple of delays, one at around 38ms and the other side around 52ms. The vocal dry up the middle with the delays (with no regeneration) on the sides gives the effect of almost double tracking.

CHORUS/FLANGER
The chorus and flanger has become one of the most used effects on clean guitars in the past 15 years. It can take a very simple part and turn it into something special. This said, don't believe for a second that putting a chorus or flanger on a guitar part will make the part right for the song. It is a tool to use. A digital flanger is a way of phasing the signal the way engineers used to do it with two tape machines, one with a varispeed on it. It changes phase relationship from 0 to 180 degrees and then on to 360.

The first time I ever heard tape phasing on a song it was "The Big Hurt," I think by Toni Fisher. It was a classic early pop track that I first heard in about 1965, then I didn't hear it again for years until the Small Faces used it in "Itchycoo Park". It was then the late 60's and any effect other than reverb was so welcome. I used tape phasing for the first time on the *Millennium* album on CBS in 1968, then again on "At the Zoo" on the album *Bookends* by Simon and Garfunkel. Reviewers have actually compared the album version to the single version and noticed that the phasing was less apparent. Since we did phasing on this album track, the singles mix in mono was done by others and had no phasing. The difference between tape phasing and flanging is very distinct to the ear. If you've never tried real tape phasing, I hope you get the chance to do it one day.

AUTO-TUNE

How many times have you heard an Antares Box used a little too much on a vocal (e.g., Cher) and it just doesn't sound real anymore? Listen to the Shania Twain album *Up*. There seems to be so much pitch correction that the character and tonality of her lead vocals are really camouflaged compared to the *Come On Over* album.

Auto-Tune can be helpful when you have a bunch of background tracks that when combined together are a bit too washy. To do an auto-tune on the tracks, do them separately to make sure that you don't use too much. I mean be careful and if in doubt use less.

Please, if you have a lead vocal that has a part out of tune then consider punching in that track with the lead singer before using a digital device to auto correct. These programs can alter the character of the lead vocal vibrato or individual style very quickly. If you do need to use one of these boxes use it for the smallest problem area not the entire track. Using Auto-Tune or Pitch Correction is a personal choice. You can use it as an effect or as a tool, just be careful on how, or should I say how much, you use.

PITCH SHIFTERS

Pitch shifters are very handy when you want to do some form of ADT. Just use the pre-delay in the unit set between 30 and 60ms and then shift the pitch up a few cents. This should give you a bit of double effect and not too much phase cancellation.

VOCODERS

Vocoder units such as the Novation Super Nova II have 42 bands, making it very clear and intelligible. To use a Vocoder you need to designate an Input or Program to be the carrier or the modulator. These units are hard to use for the first timer, but stick with it if you decide to use one. They are cool and can be an integral part of your sound design.

FILTERS AND VOLTAGE CONTROLLED FILTERS

Digital filters are on most digital products since it's the quality of these filters that make the D to A sound either good or great. If you have a good synth around your studio or even a good software version, a Voltage Controlled Filter (VCF) can be very useful to sweep on held notes. Say for instance that you have typical power chords that hold on for the whole bar then are either struck again for the next bar or change on the next chord for another four beats. If you have a VCF you can sweep these chords starting at the beginning of the bar and by the fourth beat it's filtered out a lot of the energy of the chord that will just clog the spectrum and not give much support to the track. Experiment with them, see where you can key it on to start the sweep, and see how you can enable the mix to feel alive.

VOLTAGE CONTROLLED AMPLIFIERS

VCA's can be used to set a pulse or to fade out a part or to help you make your mix move about more. Say for instance you have a semi-clean guitar playing the chords in a verse; you set a saw tooth or sine wave form to the same tempo as the song, and then use this waveform to be the modulation input to the VCA. The guitar part will pulse in time with the beat…. You can do the same thing by taking the hi-hat input, making a control voltage out of it and feeding it into the modulation input. If you cut your track to a click, use this click as the modulator input. Just a hint here, choose the depth of the effect with care.

RE-AMP

This is another way of adding life and a bit of distortion to a track of vocal, or a clean guitar or just about anything. Now the "Amp Farm" plug-in used with Pro Tools is different and used way too much; most of the time you need the physical speaker motion to really make this effect work.

Try to send the program material out to the amp at a level that closely mimics the output of a guitar. That means -20 or less. Unbalance it with a transformer box and then start to adjust the preamp settings on the amp itself. Once you achieve the desired effect out at the amp, mic it and start to mix it in with the original signal. At times no original signal will sound the best to you, other times a blend of this effect will best suit the track—it's up to your better judgment. Don't just settle for an emulated amp setting from a plug-in. Yes, these are really good these days, but real amps and real speakers can perform miracles to sounds.

CHAPTER 6

Recording the Most Important Element: Vocals

When you just finish a great take of your lead vocal, and you have the feel, where it's natural and seemingly effortless, take another take or two or three. Don't stop in between takes; select a new track and get on with it. Go through the whole tune; don't start and stop a bunch of times—think performance. As I look back, this idea of going through the whole tune, not starting and stopping several times, to some artists was so foreign.

Think performance, think of the whole, think of the linear progression of a story and how to emphasize it. I've had to push this idea on some artists I've worked with, who just wanted to start in on a vocal and stop, catch their breath, roll back a line or two and punch in... and do this throughout the entire tune. As I showed them the benefits of rolling through the whole tune four times they saw how the performance stood up from beginning to end—the energy level climaxed in the right place, it all seemed to work. Then by keeping track of which track had a problem on a particular word, I would go back and fix the word not the whole line. Combining the four tracks into one became easier for the artist to see how the energy level was the same and the intensity at any part of the song was very similar.

Lead Vocals

It is so eff ortless to do this kind of composite lead vocal that it has become a very standard/normal way of recording lead vocals. Remember earlier I said to keep notes. Well get on your computer in Excel or some spreadsheet program and put together a grid to type out the lyrics before you get in session.

Have four columns for each pass of the lead; have another column that will be your choice of the best track for that line. Lastly, add a wide column where you type in each line of the lyric. If you type in each and every line, as sung, you will find this to be a great help in keeping track of the great parts as well as the mistakes.

I used to ask the artist to listen to each track section by section and give themselves a score from 1 to 10, ten being best, of what they thought of their overall performance. Funny how, as we did this, we all picked the best components to comp together into the lead. *See illustration sample of a lyric spreadsheet.* Recording this way made the lead vocal such an event, it focused the priority in the right direction.

1	2	3	4	COMP	
					I'm hot blooded, check and see
					I got a fever of 103
					Hey Baby can you do more than dance
					I'm hot blooded, I'm hot blooded

"What should the lead singer sing to," you ask? Let me start with pitch reference. What is heard in the cans is very important to the outcome of the performance. Be sure that the guitars are in tune and as they get louder and with more crunch that there is some element of the chord (something with the third included) present in this phone mix. When you sing with phones you get a pressure sensation to the extent that pops and thumps you don't hear in the control room will be present in the cans. As you put together this mix for the singer to use, make sure you listen to what they are hearing on the same brand of phones. This way you will be sure of the pitch reference you're sending to the studio.

Next is "foldback," the amount of the mic that is fed through the console and with added effects sent back to the singer for reference. There is a pretty wide window of acceptance level here that will serve the singer with a good mix of the tracks and enough of themselves to get excited and perform. But there is also a danger, if there is too much vocal going back, the singer can sing flat. If there is too little they could sing sharp.

Have you ever put on headphones and listened to the track and without any foldback of your own voice and heard people in the room plugging their ears in horror because you're singing so out of tune? Think of the foldback level as a tuner—down is up and up is down. The more foldback level you feed, the flatter the vocalist. The less you feed, the sharper the vocalist. The better the singer, the less this has an effect on pitch since they are so in tune to their own body that they are listening to bone contact more than foldback. It's just one of those natural things. If all else fails, tell the singer that they need to lift one headphone slightly off the ear, so they can hear themselves more directly in the room.

LATENCY

Now here is an issue that has confronted us since the first day of recording within a computer or on digital consoles. There is a time delay going through A to D converters of about a millisecond. Some people have told me that there is no way a vocalist can record with a millisecond delay from what they sing to what is returned to their cans. They say there will be a comb filter effect in their head from the source to the sound returning in their cans. Well remember I said earlier that a millisecond is about 13 inches.

Think about all the vocals that were cut for years on analog equipment without this latency but the singer stood 13 inches away from the mic. My math says that there should be the same comb filter effect here too. This form of latency hasn't affected recordings so far and it probably won't in the future, especially if you're careful. Lastly, put some effects such as a bit of reverb, delay, compression etc. on the vocal you send back to the floor; all in all, the sound of the vocal is now processed a bit and the singer will more than likely look at it as a help and not a hindrance.

INTELLIGIBILITY OF THE LEAD VOCAL

Pronunciation is a trying ordeal when recording a lead vocal. So many times a vocalist will trigger their tonality on a vowel sound that's easy for them, where they can hear themselves and pitch properly. I've had several artists that were not natural singers, but very good vocal coaches trained them. These coaches can get more out of you than you can imagine.

There was one coach that had a warm-up exercise using just sounds repeated on the lowest tone you could sing. Warm up your voice with a single low note... HUN GAH WEEE AH, take a breath, then go up a half a tone and repeat HUN GAH WEEE AH very slowly. Then continue up the chromatic scale… start as low as you can and go as high as you can. Note how the EEE sound starts resonating in your sinus cavities? A simple vocal warm-up trick, but the real trick is to remember that feeling and how your voice got there. Once you get this resonance, try to place your vocal in the same part of your throat. You'll be amazed at how much easier it will be to understand what you're singing about. The overall vocal sound you get is directly proportional to the performance given by your vocalist. If there is intelligibility, then with proper mic technique and not too much compression or other effects *the lyric* will definitely be heard.

Background Vocals

Many times I listen to tracks that I like and I'm always so amazed by some of the background vocal layering done today. It's not uncommon to hear more than two-part harmony layered with dozens of tracks. That sound of the layering is just so cool.

When you start to do background vocal work on your track, look to the Lead Vocal and find a spot where it does not command total attention. Here is a point of reference, a starting point for yet another composition within a composition. A melody, a new phrasing of the key line in the lyric, or total departure from the structure and existing melody might be necessary. Anything is possible, and more than likely it will come to you quickly when you just look at the obvious. Is the chorus building, does it need vocal strengthening? Once you've made an entrance with BG vocals, do they need to enter again in the next verse or pre chorus?

There are, of course, no exact rules to follow here, but you will know where they are needed. Most of your favorite hits have followed a bit of formula, and you can too. If you find your parts sounding generic, work some more at it to complete the picture. I would always try to have at least one moment within a song where the BG vocals were so necessary and once you heard the track with them in this spot you would think "How'd I ever live without them?" Here's a moment for you to break out of the generic and get a bit weird, it's probably OK. Some of the time the strength of basic BG vocals will be enough. This too is totally OK. The composition or complexity is yours to decide.

Overdubbing

As you're building your track, get a vocal on it as soon as possible, even if it's just a good rough. The vocal is the song, so as you're overdubbing keyboards, guitars, and who knows what other stuff you've come up with, you can be sure you're not covering that important hook lyric line. Doubling of some parts is cool especially if they are placed hard left and hard right, but if they are too identical, you've created ultra mono. I used to do what I would call *soft doubles* on rhythm guitars, so within the takes they would vary enough to be really interesting. When you start to layer in a synth part, be careful of the massive size prevalent with some factory sounds. Sometimes these sounds are so big that they make the rest of the track sound small, at least at the level the synth needs to be at to be heard. Try looking for sounds with a range of overtones that complement and don't conflict with your vocals and guitars. Try taking a sound and running it through a Leslie, mic it in stereo and this way it won't take up too much room in the mix.

Too many parts can also be hell when you start mixing. A little of this, a little of that, and pretty soon there is a little of everything, you know… no focus or simplicity or especially groove. Think of how your favorite artist structures the overdubbing on their tracks, where everything complements what just went past or is just coming up. Classic simplicity is the key, where there is never a time where the listener can't hear everything on the track.

Lead Solos or Features

Does it need this release from the vocal? Does the solo instrument fit the song? Does the solo seem too long or too short? Is it just showing off or is the melody really solidified? These are all questions you need to ask yourself before accepting any solo arranged into the track, so you need to ask yourself these questions very early on in this process.

OK, you've arranged into the song this solo section; and the guitar player is just coming up with flashy riffs that have no relationship to the tune, or the genre, or sometimes to music itself. What to do? Let's start with instrument selection. Look to your strength in musicianship—it usually will show the way. If you're a great guitar player or you have a great player in the band, let them be the source of the creativity. Look to the writers of the song—they can guide the melodic content.

If you have a great keyboard player maybe the instrument of choice is not the guitar. It's the musicianship that counts. Now is the structure over a verse, or chorus, or is it a completely new section? This should guide you toward the emphasis that needs to be placed on the sound. If it's over a verse, does the chord strength fit the tone? If it's over a chorus, is there too much going on to relate to the solo as a feature?

I'm asking questions to make you think of the possibilities. If you choose the right elements to support the solo then you can guide the sound to match the intensity, make sense? Does the next section following the solo need to climax the hook of the song? Does the solo smoothly end or segue into this section? Does it cover important vocal melody lines? Or do you just need to edit out the part? Just be careful and think of the whole picture as you approach the solo and all will end well.

Final Ideas Before Completion

Oh, those final overdubs. The tambourine parts, the shakers, the cow bell, you know, the stuff you might need in the mix. Never feel like something you put on a track is gospel truth and has to be heard. Those final days of fiddling around without pressure knowing that the song is really good and a little experimentation are sure fun. Your hard work, energy, and dedication have earned you the right to mess around with some last minute ideas. Don't get too involved but go ahead and take some time to get a new perspective.

CHAPTER 7

Speakers

Before I get on to mixing, the next few pages touch on the subject of speakers, and how you are listening. The accuracy of what and how you hear is going to be close to 50% of the outcome of your project. Hearing really is believing; and if you're being fooled in your own studio, what do you think is going to happen elsewhere?

Monitor Speakers vs. Reference Monitors

Why is it called a monitor? Studio monitors are there to let you hear an accurate representation of what you're recording. If the monitor isn't telling you the truth about what you're listening to then it's just a speaker not a *reference monitor*. Speakers are designed to have a tonal character. Some have a very bright sound; others supply an abundance of bottom end. Let the listener at home choose from what seems like millions of consumer products. You want accuracy and the only way to get it is with a system that has been designed to be a true reference. I think I sound like a commercial, well maybe, but the truth in knowing what you are hearing is so valuable. If you don't know what you're hearing, you might as well be mixing with earplugs.

Sounds Great? That May Not Be the Right Choice.

The wrong way to buy monitors is to take a CD with you to the store and listen for the best sounding speaker. Sure, this is great if you're looking for a pair of speakers to listen to music on, but that's not why you're buying the monitors. Reference monitors are tools that are used like a surgeon uses a scalpel. Making a great recording is hard enough; your dedication requires precision and accuracy. Let's at least know that any decision you make is based on your artistic preferences not on the coloration of what you're listening to. Sure, it's harder to make a record without the hype of a speaker, but at the end of the day you'll finish up with a recording that sounds awesome, the way you wanted it to, regardless of what it's played back on. Remember what I stated earlier, your audience is the record buyer and he has his system that he knows and has a sonic memory of what it sounds like.

How to Demo a Studio Monitor

This is the toughest part of the whole selection process. How do you listen to and compare monitors when you don't have the benefit of a known? It's like test-driving a car with a blindfold on. In other words, how do you know which speaker will make a better monitor? Well, this is where your listening skills come into play, and believe me, it's something you will work on all your life, so don't expect to be an expert the first time out. Critical listening takes practice and patience, so make sure you prepare for the visit to the store so that you can get the most out of the trip.

Listen for the *detail* in a particular instrument, then on the same recording the apparent level of the vocal on speaker "A" then on speaker "B." Then listen for the subtleties of percussive sounds at different levels between the two speaker samples. There are no hard and fast rules to go, by merely guidelines. Just don't expect to show up and listen for the "best sounding" speaker, or you'll likely leave disappointed, and if you buy a system, you'll probably be returning it to the store in a week or so.

Stereo Monitor Placement

Whether you use a console or a mouse to record you need to stay in the sweet spot if you're going to mix effectively. The sweet spot is that region of space where the sound from each of your monitors reaches your ears at equal intensity. Well, that's really only half the story. The other half is that the phase relationship between the monitors has to be equal and consistent. Phase is affected by the number and positioning of the drivers inside the speaker cabinet (something you can't do anything about) and by the way that the speakers are positioned (the thing you can do something about). Remember that table or console in front of you is a reflector and will cause first reflection phase anomalies.

Half-space, Whole-space, Outer space

When a speaker reproduces low frequency sounds it tends to radiate those sounds omni directionally. What this means is simply that the speaker throws low frequency sounds out in all directions, including front, back, sides and top. As you can imagine, much of this sound is going somewhere other than right at the listener, positioned right in front of the speaker. If a speaker were hanging in mid-air then we would say it is in whole space, without touching any boundaries. The listener would then hear only what is being directed out of the front of the speaker. If the same speaker were placed on a solid wall, then half of the low frequency sound that was going off into space will now be reflected back at the listener and the sound would be perceived as having more bass.

That's a result of what the technical boys call the "boundary effect" and it's the first thing you need to know about speaker placement. Be careful with those little bass roll-off filter switches on the back of so many active monitors; they are set at a particular frequency and roll off at a set rate. Did they come to your room and measure how far away from the wall your speakers are sitting? I think not. But in knowing this, don't go crazy; give your monitor a solid footing to work from. I mean, mount it well, not just on a pole stand, but also something with some mass to it. The speaker voice coil is a motor that puts a lot of air in motion at low frequencies. Give the monitor a chance to work.

Subwoofers

Let's start out by looking at the definition of a subwoofer. A subwoofer is a speaker that extends the low-frequency limit of a sound system's frequency response. It's not there to make the bass that much louder. In recording however, the subwoofer is there to make the very bottom octaves audible that you probably couldn't hear out of your smaller main monitors. That is until you start to deliver in 5.1 or other surround formats, then the sub-woofer is there for a completely different reason. Using a subwoofer in a stereo mixing situation is very difficult. The crossover point is probably around 80 Hz; think of that low E on the guitar… that's 82 Hz, so part of the low E is coming from the main monitor in front of you and some has been redirected to the subwoofer over in the corner someplace.

Active or Passive?

Do you really need another piece of equipment (the power amplifier) in your studio? Aside from the simple convenience, why buy monitors with amplifiers built in as opposed to buying speakers and a separate amplifier? We see advertisements making vivid claims of this—speakers being so flat and accurate etc. then there's the real reason. The ads will tell you that an active system matches the right amplifier to the speakers for optimum performance. While this is sometimes true, more often it disguises the fact that integrated electronics allows a manufacturer to make nearly any driver: cheap, under-sized, stamped steel or plastic, made in some offshore country by underpaid slaves, and held together with staples and bad glue, sound decent when they add tons of electronic equalization. Even a poorly designed speaker can be made to sound acceptable with the right amount of electronic trickery. But what does all of that electronic manipulation do to the integrity of the original music? Well, I'll tell you, it makes it harder and harder to really know what you're listening to, in fact letting technology get in the way of your creativity.

Room Acoustics

When you set up your room did you realize that 50% of what you're hearing is the room itself? If you paid for all this high definition equipment then why aren't you listening in a treated room that will allow the clarity and articulation to be heard? The first reflection point in any room is the most critical. It's the point where the direct vs. reflected sounds from the speaker converge at the listening position. This mode is very detrimental to accurate reproduction of any sound. If you have purchased equipment for your own studio, make sure you use an accurate system to acoustically treat the room.

You must locate and treat the first reflection points in your listening environment. To find this first reflection point, sit in your listening position in front of your mixer or where you create. Have a friend take a mirror and place it flat against say the left wall. As your friend moves the mirror horizontally along the wall, find the place where you first see the left speaker; that locates the first reflection point. Make sure there is wide band treatment at that exact location. Repeat this whole procedure for the right wall and then the ceiling. Oh and when I say wide band, I mean some form of acoustic panel that works down to 250Hz.

This is all part of that direct vs. reflected sound wave stuff. If sound travels at a set rate... the sound that bounces off that left wall arrives at your ears later than the direct sound from the speaker. You don't hear it as delay, since it's probably only about 3 to 5 ms, but inside your head you get this comb filter effect that will cancel out certain frequencies to varying degrees. So what you're hearing is not what you're getting. Is it simple enough to spot the trouble points? If you don't take some measures, you could spend months and months working on getting the room even as close as 60% correct.

Look around your room and take notes as to several problem areas. That is, are the walls parallel? Do you have a lot of glass? Is the ceiling just another parallel surface to the floor? Is the floor concrete, wood, carpeted? The time you take making sure what you're hearing is what you're getting is invaluable. Gone are the days when you can put "egg cartons" or "cut foam" up on the walls. The technology available is very high tech and very high definition. Choose professional solutions to treat your room, look for a system that has engineering skill and real world aptitude closely intertwined. I think I've used this phrase several times now—*get help*! The more time an engineer or producer spends in the studio the more apt he will be to spot trouble areas and maybe even know of a solution.

I hope I've made myself clear during this chapter. You want a reference monitor that tells you the truth, not a monitor that just sounds good to you, played back in an acoustic environment that suits the quality of the monitor. And can be relied upon to tell you the truth. It's hard to turn your back on some of the amplified monitors out in the world today. They sound great on first listen. The small Genelec is hyped a tiny bit on the top end to sound crisp. The Mackie lacks definition of the midrange and it's very hard to define the bottom even though it sounds wonderful. The Event and KRK's are too different from unit to unit. You could line up 10 of each of these monitors in a row and probably not find two that have the same coloration of sound. And the list goes on and on. You need to have a reference that you know and trust. I mean that *you* know and *you* trust to be able to make the everyday decisions on performance, placement, volume, and spectrum. Look to quality companies with quality professional products, put them in an acoustically treated room and that combination will end up being your best investment.

CHAPTER 8

Mixing

Let's talk about doing everything in your computer. With all that CPU power you can natively record, sequence, modify, use plug-ins to get even more specialized effects, set up a mixer build a "virtual channel strip," and on and on.

This is the not the new way to record and mix, it's just another way to record and mix. Don't listen to anyone who calls using a large or small format mixer "Old-School" or "Old Fashioned"—they are definitely wrong. If you don't believe me, or think I'm old fashioned for even saying that, fade down some music on your built-in CD player on your computer. If you're on a PC go down to the lower right hand corner of the screen and click on the little speaker icon, then while the music is playing, try to fade down *smoothly*. I bet you can't at the very bottom, and there will be a couple of hiccups in the middle. Yes, you can do it all on the desktop monitor, but if there is a control surface available to you, use it and make the mix as much a part of the overall performance as the playing of each instrument or singing of each vocal.

Let's think of this mixing console as a "Time Honored" method of mixing. Take four channels of background vocals, a lead vocal and a secondary lead vocal and run the song. Do a ride, do that ultimate blend in real time that makes the lyric, melody and arrangement just pop out of the speakers. You just can't do that with a mouse, it's one fader at a time, and trying to sync that blend over a whole song could take you hours and still not be perfect.

You may say, "why not just group the faders and then do a single mouse ride?" This is true, you can do this, but what about the times where you want to pinch a bit more of track 3 during the pre chorus, etc.?

It's all up to your personal preference, although I'm all for the performance of the mix itself. Moving touch sensitive fader automation is very helpful when it comes to more complex mixes with more than 24 tracks or elements. The mix is just another performance and can be the difference between being heard and not being heard.

The Big Picture

It's all about human feel, even in the mix, or should I say, especially in the mix. The final mix is what you present to all the factions out there in A&R, record company, radio, MTV, and most importantly, consumer-land. Now that we all agree that the final mix is very important, let's look to the big picture.

Never forget the feeling you got when you first wrote or heard the song—that feeling is the reason you recorded the song in the first place. What are the elements that interested you the most? Why did you use this guitar part, that rhythm part, this keyboard pad, that bass line? It's all about prioritization. You're not just blending, you are setting up the way the listener will interpret your sound, your song, and your musicianship.

Spectral Mixing

Spectral mixing is a technical term that describes this tonal separation methodology. When you start mixing, do you start with the drums? If you do, which drum do you start with?

I hear so many mixes where they start with the kick drum and make it so big that inevitably all the other sounds suffer around it. Put each element into its own little box first. Do a ruff mix on the drums; add the bass, and then the rest of the rhythm section. After you have re-created that feel of the original basic track, *then* go into the individual elements and do with them what you like. Shave a bunch off here, boost in an area where the tonality is weak there, trim, trim, trim, but always going back and forth between that original and your newfound mix. This way you will not lose track of the big picture.

To begin, see the whole in your mind's eye, think of the potential of the sum of the parts. Put yourself into the listener's position and listen as if it was the first time. The whole spectrum is in front of you. Think of the space the vocal range will take up in your mix. Remember it is the most important element. As you listen, look at your analyzer to see how the midrange builds when the human voice is present. Now go back to the beginning and start to put together the elements to best suit the genre. In doing this you will find that there should be a hole in the middle of your spectrum, where the midrange doesn't build up. Place your vocal into this space. If intelligibility is still a problem you've added too many other colors into this area of the mix.

"Too big," you say? Maybe you think I'm crazy and wonder how can something be too big. The way you present the rhythm section is the foundation of the mix. You've heard mixes where everything sits in such a cool place within the whole of the mix. This is what you're striving to emulate. Pick one of these mixes you love to listen to, have it on the return selection of your desk, keep going back and forth, sure it's a different song, different arrangement, but listen to the way the spectrum is filled. If you have that spectrum analyzer, put it on memory A for the CD and memory B for your mix. Then study the differences. Dissect your mix once again looking to where you equalized instruments and layered in other elements to see where there could be a buildup.

This all sounds complex and perplexing at best, but this too will come easier the more experience you have. To look at a mix, sonically dissect it, and make your corrections and other decisions quickly is all part of the art of mixing. There are always a lot of questions to ask yourself: is there too much of the drums, does this overpower the rest of the track, is it way too complex for the listener to comprehend on first listen? Is too much stuff floating around within the mix? Is it too dry? Is it too wet? Is the vocal distinct? What is the first thing your ear is drawn to? Does it convey the message of the song? Are there conflicting tones or phrases? Does the sum of all the parts make up a whole or is it overstuffed? Today's mixes can be so open and simple that when you put an effect on a vocal it is the most important thing you do.

Choose carefully and investigate the possibilities, then apply cautiously.

Stereo vs. Surround

Most of the mixes you'll do today are two-channel stereo. I'm talking about simple left/right, straight ahead mixing that we've been listening to for years. Although this is the normal for most releases, as time marches on and home theater becomes more and more installed into homes, you'll find more and more demand for surround product.

The film business has had a lock on this surround delivery format for over a decade now and they know that the surround sound field is so necessary when it comes to the "theater" experience. As listeners invest more money into their own surround sound systems they want to be able to enjoy the benefits of 5.1 surround sound in their music too. Someday this will be a big deal at record companies and they will have a new marketing and sales channel to work and hopefully profit from.

Now there are many ways to set up your room for surround work. I can give you some hints to help keep you on track. The main thing to think about is where the mix will be played back and on what. Most of the time it's going to be in a living room, family room or den set up with three speakers across the front and two in the back. This placement of the rear speakers is a point of conjecture between several different camps. Should the rear speakers be set up 110 degrees from center as Dolby states? Or should the rear speakers be set up definitively in the rear at 130 to 150 degrees around from center? The choice is yours, pretty much dictated by your room and where you *can* put them. Remember though that the end customer will probably only be able to set the five speakers up where it works in his room, such as on the back wall pointing down to the couch, that's right up against the back wall. Or worse yet he will only be able to set up the speakers where his wife lets him, she'll say, "Two speakers were bad enough, now there are five, and what's that big box over in the corner?"

So once again use your best judgment; if your gear will let you pan a surround image, and the front three speakers are the same in quality, you'll probably be OK. Search the Internet and read the information and even message board threads on several web sites on placement, then just try out what works for your room, since this is what the listener at their home will do. Included on the companion Web site for this book (http://www.courseptr.com/downloads) is a pdf copy of Dolby's document named "5.1 Channel Music Production Guidelines," which will give you a wealth of information.

I want to stick my two cents in here as far as placement in your room and where you sit at your control console. The consumer doesn't sit in the near field; in fact he sits probably almost eight feet away from the front speakers. So do you set up the three speakers across the front of your desk? No probably not.

Try this on for size. Place your mixer, computer or whatever it is, so your listening position is 55% of the depth of the room you're in. This means pull your desk away from that pesky front wall. Place the speakers on stands so you emulate a "home theater." In doing this you have eliminated a couple of problem areas when it comes to your reference monitors, and that is the reflection off the face of the desk and the boundary effect off the back wall. Now you've created a playback field very close to how your customer (that listener in the home) will ultimately listen to your mixes.

I remember when studios tried to emulate a car radio speaker to mix down to. They even had door panels or front dashboards taken off Chevys placed in their control rooms. This is all well and good to have another frame of reference, but just think how different your car sounds to the next car you sit in. You just can't preconceive how your product will be played. Thankfully the listener has a sonic memory of what his home theater, stereo, or car sounds like to him; it's his normal listening environment, and only his. And finally the listener is listening to more of the performance than what made his stereo sound good.

The Dot One Channel

What do I do with all of this bass I have available? Do I try to use this channel for the entire bottom end? Quick answer is *no*. The dot one channel is for Low Frequency Effects. The Bass Management System in the end user's receiver will direct most of the bottom under 80 Hz to this subwoofer and add in the LFE. When you're mixing, if you don't have full range monitors, be sure to use a bass management box of some kind.

If you try to put too much into this channel you'll be chancing an overload within the bit stream of most DVD decoders. The LFE channel is to be used for just that, low frequency effects, the ones that don't happen that often, but when they do, you want to give the listener a bigger bang.

Stereo Panning

Here is an area where I see so many young engineers get into that finite placement in the left-right image or sound stage. As you start to place all of the elements of your project, think about where they are in relationship to "reality"—I mean where they would be placed if the "band" was right there in front of you, on stage. This is a good place to start. I've seen and heard so many mixes where you just can't differentiate where things are placed: 5 degrees left of center, 7 degrees farther left of center and on and on. What so many engineers and producers end up with is glorious semi-mono. The ear can only tell the difference of *about* 7 placements from left to right; therefore, if you have hard left, center, and hard right, there are only four other placements that the ear can actually perceive with any accuracy.

When you place instruments and vocals within these three main areas: left, center, and right, you're already ahead of the game. With today's MIDI implementation of panning in sequencers and Digital Audio Workstation, there are 127 positions left of center and 127 positions right of center. Don't get into this degree of sophistication; just use your ears and then look at the numbers and you'll get a firm understanding of what I'm talking about. No one can hear the difference between MIDI position L91 and MIDI position L92.

Surround Panning

Surround panning is another animal altogether. As you listen to other surround mixes, you'll find that the ones that make a defined statement of putting you either on the stage or inside of a "total" experience will have the most impact. Too much movement is distracting to the listener; they want to enjoy the music not get dizzy. Be careful and realize that you'll hate the first 10 or 15 surround mixes you do. I know I did. Keep at it, go and listen to other albums mixed in surround and take notes on how and where they did the panning and placement. It's a good place to start. Now go ahead and do what you want—the same rules will apply. Less is more when it comes to tricky panning in stereo or surround sound.

I had the pleasure of hearing a surround mix by Bob Clearmountain where he took a sub-mix of the rhythm section and during a solo started to slowly rotate this sub-mix from the left/right clockwise to the right/right rear then on to the right rear/left rear etc. It was one of the most clever and "effective" feature pannings I've ever heard. Congratulations Bob on a great idea, which is very hard to do.

Overall Compression

Now here is a good challenge. Where should you try to tighten up the track, on the final output or within the groups? Where possible, try to do this *"tighten up"* at a group level first. Say for instance, you have an 8-bus desk that has group faders with inserts and assignments back to the L/R mix. Use this patch point! Assign all the drums (panned the way you want them) and the bass to a pair of sub-masters. Then insert a two-channel compressor across this stereo group. As you adjust the settings to allow some of the transients to pass through, note how the drums and bass become a "package" that's tight and working together.

For those of you where you don't have sub-group insert points, you can always try program compression at the final insert point just before the master fader.

Remember this can alter your entire mix so don't put it across the mix when you first start or else you'll be fighting against this compressor whenever you want something to jump out of your mix. Some of the subtleties will be minimized, so use it with care, since you can add this afterwards with the same outcome. Be careful not to lock yourself into the sound of this compressor while printing to two-track; the guy at the mastering house just might have a unit that sounds much better. But be aware that doing it at mastering is after the master fade, so any effect of tight compression will be lost as soon as the program level drops below the threshold point of this mastering compressor.

Surround compression is a bit different. Make sure you link all five channels together so your image doesn't shift. There will be times when the kick drum in the center channel will overpower the rest of the channels, and you may want to not have any compression at all in some of these instances. The best and only real way to accomplish this is to use *your ears*.

What Do I Mix Down To?

This is always important to look at; it's the finality of the project. Will the method that you've chosen be around just a few years from now? If you're mixing to a computer can you get the mix off easily onto a format that you can play? What happens if the computer crashes? Do you have a backup that doesn't suffer from generation loss? I'm planting these seeds in hopes that you will mix down to several formats either simultaneously or at least be diligent in making zero loss copies onto several formats as soon as each mix is finished. You just never know when the next thing that you do will crash or fragment a disk and blow the work you've already done.

Once again, I trust that you will back up everything often. Try getting your mix to an analog machine if possible, even if it's after the fact. An analog generation can take a digital mix and really add that warmth and harmonic distortion that sounds great. Then just think, once you're on analog, you can use any sample rate you want and it's a great way to get the final product to 16 bit 44.1 CD standards without going through sample rate converters. If you think that you can't hear sample rate converters work, just think of the math they are doing. Divide by this, throw away that, resample this, and then shoot it out the output. There is a difference. Best thing here is to use your ears and what you've learned to help you decide which way is the best for your project.

CHAPTER 9

Competition Is Fierce— Collaboration Is Cool

Anyone who has gone to the well and tried to bring up a full bucket of water on the first try will usually be a very frustrated person. There are times when you have to say, "Hey, I need some help!" These will probably be the most important words you've ever spoken. Knowing when to ask for that uncanny expertise to help within a lyric, within a melody, or even within an arrangement, are the facts of life when it comes to music.

I think that artists who work and create with others have a much more diverse catalog in the end. They just have so much more to offer, you know, no weaknesses. This is the grandest example of strength in numbers. Collaboration is very cool. There are so many others out there ready to claw their way to the top. It's just great anytime you can prop yourself up with some extra know-how.

I always looked at those overnight successes as if they were really just one more work in progress. If you're a guitar player, do you practice eight hours a day? If you're a vocalist, do you sing eight hours a day? Well, do you sing at least enough to drive anyone crazy? Even with this kind of dedication there just isn't enough time in the day to really get *great* at everything you want to do. It just takes too much time and energy. Wait a minute—this is "overnight?"

Know your strengths and recognize your weaknesses.

▶ Identify the likes and dislikes of your listener.

▶ Do your homework within the genre you choose to work in.

▶ Perfect your art (this could take years).

▶ Learn how to effectively market your art (this too could take years).

Know Your Audience

Pick your demographic, pick your genre, apply your intelligence toward it and cut your tunes. You've been to clubs, you listen to the radio, you watch MTV, and all are the research vehicles you need to observe and know your audience. Remember the first audience is usually the *record company;* they are the ones that listen first, and you have to get by their super critical ears to get anywhere. Don't force a tune or special part of a song down the record company's throat; it will always come back to haunt you even if you're right. Ego plays a huge role with artists, producers, and at the record company; they all want to take credit for the hit and all want to place the blame for the miss. Keep your music radio- and promotion-friendly with your ideas and sound wherever possible; this just gives you a leg up on the competition.

Ah, yes, the competition, this band and that band, male singers, female singers, hip hop, R&B, Trance, etc. they all have their loyal followers, and their favorite sons. There are over 5,000 bands in Southern California all struggling for the five or six major record company annual slots for release. There's the same situation in Nashville with thousands of artists vying for the few available contracts each year. New York is overflowing with so many super-talented people; it's crazy. And then there's everywhere in between those three major music regions.

Now certainly there is more than one record company, but there are only a few major labels and a whole bunch of independents, relatively few of which produce tangible successful record sales. Today's global economic restraints, illegal downloading of files, and lagging retail record sales, have made major and independent labels alike tighten their belts again and again to help stave off the accountants. Somewhere there has to be the cash to pay for the infrastructure, recording, and signing costs. This cash comes from record sales at retail for the most part. TV and catalog sales attribute a sizable portion, but at the end of it all, it really is all about the retail record store. Therefore don't ever think that it doesn't matter if any record sells. Look at the costs involved with recording, marketing, manufacturing and distribution of any one album.

Let's take a snapshot of the approximate costs facing the record companies today. First there are the signing costs; including legal fees and administration let's say that's $50,000. Second is the recording budget, say it's $150,000. Third are the monstrous marketing costs (this covers videos, advertisements in the trades or on TV, promotional goods, design costs, free goods in the stores to stock the record, etc.), another $250,000. Then toss in the cost of tour support, travel, and now the big one, money for the indie promotion. When you add this up it totals nearly $1,000,000. This is the reality of the type of investment it takes to seriously sign an artist and then create, record, market, and promote their recording by nationally distributed record label. Wow, does it make fiscal sense to make records when 25% or more of all your fans will download the product for free? So did I say competition is fierce? You bet it is. This million-dollar scenario is at the majors and this is what they are trying to get a handle on right now.

There are other ways to get your music out to the listeners, and it won't cost a million dollars to do it, like local promotion in a geographic area of the country. Regional hits can pay the bills and keep your dream alive. There are ways to keep pushing upward with a regional hit that can take on the majors in that region. Do you think that might get the attention of the majors? When all else fails, with the right web site and some local TV coverage, a touring band can break through with a strong fan base leading the charge. I have seen it happen where a band just doesn't give up, keeps plugging away, and the rest is history.

Promotion

Market awareness is paramount, not just to the record company, but especially to you the artist or producer. The look of your marketing is crucial to the way the end customer will pick up on your music. When it comes time to market your art, it's not only about the song, music, etc. but it's about the look. It's about the way you present the whole package. Look to see what is being done to promote your competition, then formulate a plan, stick to it and see it through. Don't have such lofty ideas that no one will be able to implement your plan. Make it simple but clever!

I once was involved in a comedy album. You know, the ones that never see the light of day at the record company. The artist and I put together a plan to get the attention of the record company. We went out and secured a parade permit for the street to the side of their offices for noontime on a Friday. Then we hired an elephant and trainer, bought 20 pounds of peanuts and 100 small brown paper lunch bags, filled the bags with the peanuts and stapled a note on the bag that said, *"You signed me for peanuts now come outside at noon and feed my elephant."*

I'll tell you, we got tons of coverage on the local news, and got everyone at the label talking about those crazy guys that ran around the office throwing bags of peanuts at everybody. The whole thing cost $500. The album had some life where it had no chance before. So be clever, do the impossible, but keep your costs down.

A second year marketing/communications student could have written some of the marketing plans I've seen at labels. The way to make an impression is to actually write out your plan and when you deliver the album, deliver the plan. You're not dictating what you expect to be done, just making a bunch of suggestions; state that fact on the front page. Make the plan have at least three tiers.

▶ Tier 1—Start with a simple launch plan to radio, TV, press, and live appearance. Make yourself or the artist available for "phoners" and anything else you can do to keep your record in front of the promo department. Don't be a pest, just help whenever possible. The promo department will actually appreciate it.

▶ Tier 2—Here's where the money comes in for things such as ad design and placement, web design and hosting, then that expensive must-have video. Make sure you've already done some homework with video directors and crews so you can give an educated *estimate* of what it will cost. Do your own storyboard suggestions for the video. Sit down with some "known" directors and talk about your song and ask for ideas. List the number of sets that will have to be built and or locations that will have to be contacted and secured. List the approximate editing time to get it done after shooting. And always give amount of dollars spent in each category and give a total. Present this to the label and if it's within their budget you'll have a better chance of doing the video.

▶ Tier 3—This is almost as costly; it has to do with national support of a tour, national support of radio station personal appearances, indie promotion and god only knows what else. If tiers 1 and 2 have paid off in showings of the video or stations are adding your single, this is when the almighty buck comes in to play. When the return on the investment they made in promotion starts happening, this will tell the labels the time is right for this level of promotional investment in your recording and career.

You must know that a priority release from a label seems to get the full push right off the bat. It seems that as soon as its released, stations all over the place pick it up, even if it's a totally unknown artist. Who decides? Where does this artist come from? Where is the power coming from? Usually it comes from the top. That's when a record is pushed so hard that the media itself is the messenger. People will line up to buy the record. And then all of a sudden, come the rave reviews as to how great this new artist is.

How did it happen so fast, you ask? Well, so much of American radio is programmed by so few people that if a record gets this priority push directly to these program-mers it could hit almost overnight. But this takes money and commitment. I'm not saying it's all payola; more specifically I'm saying that when this record hits these programmers it is with the "total commitment" of the label. This way the programmer knows that the label will follow through with all their promises. Nudge nudge, wink wink.

Today, it is just as hard as it has ever been to get your record played or your song cut and most likely even harder than that! Consolidation of the majors, big com-pany politics and buying placement on albums, these are only the beginning of where the total commitment from your label starts. But these are the ways to break through today. Just look to the consolidation of radio. Clear Channel owns so many of the radio stations across the US that to get on the air you have to use indie pro-motion and this can run into tens or even hundreds of thousands of dollars. More of the "nudge nudge, wink wink." What is the new artist, producer, or songwriter to do? Well it breaks down to that same old adage: song, performance, sound, and then *tenacious self-promotion.*

For the writers amongst us there are a very few inde-pendent companies such as Taxi that perform a pretty good service in pitching your songs. They have subscrip-tion fees that cost you some money, but it's not an arm and a leg. They can make a bit of a difference, but don't rely on them alone. You've got to network within your friends and fellow writers/musicians. You never know when a friend needs some help on a song that they might perform in a club somewhere and gets heard by someone who works at a label, film company, or the like. Maybe the act gets signed; maybe the film company likes the genre, but needs a "custom" product. It's all about getting out there and pushing, not just to the stars and majors, but network to anyone and everyone.

The publishing company deals with promotion all the time, too. Some of the things that they do are very clever, some straight out payoffs. I once heard of a producer that would only cut a tune for one of his big artists if he got a sizable amount of cash under the table from the publisher. If I was the artist, I would be horrified and disillusioned to say the least. These are more of the facts of life in the record business. So what is an unknown to do? How do you break through? I'll tell you a great song really helps along with three simple words: dedication, dedication, and more dedication.

EPK (Electronic Press Kit)

Have you ever seen this work? It is cheap to distribute, but what is the percentage of influential people at record labels that will take the time to actually open it? I have never completely read through one of them, other than look at a few pictures and scan the reviews in them. There just isn't enough time. For the new artists and producers, a few companies offer promotion services if you press your CD with them, like Oasis CD. Here's an opportunity to get further along in the startup plan. Getting on a sampler CD is good if you can do it without paying a fee. Getting some play at indie radio is great. But selling some product in stores and having the sales uploaded to the SoundScan database is even better.

Independent radio is a small grassroots mode of promotion, and the majors will sometimes laugh at the statistics because it really is a small percentage of listeners. But just ask some of the artists that have had the persistence to stick it out. The common thread in all artists, producers and songwriters is that drive to succeed. It is a very necessary component.

CHAPTER 10

Royalties—What a Concept

To take little or no money up front and bet everything you have or will have in the near future on somebody out there in record-store-land actually buying enough of your records to make sense—that's the real gamble. We all will do it because of ego or because our music is the coolest or whatever. It's just one of those things you can't deny.

Royalties can and will someday come back to give extra meaning to you and your family. Knowing that people are actually buying your inspiration, enough people in fact bought your creativity to add up to an amount of money that won't embarrass or depress you when you go to the bank with the check to cash it—that's the final reward. It's satisfaction in the knowledge that your music is salable, commercial, unique enough to really make a difference, and then on top of everything others are listening to your music. Maybe even change or affect their lives. Even more payoff, this is great isn't it?

Just protect yourself from the snakes out there as in most any business. You remember the blind rabbit and blind snake joke right? If not go to the back of the book, I've put it in the Glossary. Royalties have been paid to performers, producers, and writers for generations. And in some cases it was the only reward for all the time and energy put into a project.

Now let's take a look at the royalty statements. Did you know that most record company contracts are written so that the company doesn't have to account if the sales are less than x units, whatever small number that may be? But what do they have to do if you sell 500 records every six months for six years? They still have to account to you and write you a check, even if those 6,000 records were sold 10 years after the original record deal.

If you're the publisher as well as the artist, here's a good set of checks and balances you can look at to compare statements and accounting. Mistakes can be made and it's usually not in your favor. To come to the defense of the record company look at the enormous task they have accounting for sales of all the albums they've ever released. What's been returned by stores, what's free goods for promotion, catalog sales, compilation sales—the list goes on and on. And to send out statements twice a year. Wow! It's really a huge undertaking. But usually this works very well and the rewards are sizable.

All I can say is, be judicious and consult a lawyer before you sign anything. You are an artist, not a lawyer. I've seen some insane deals signed by managers, artists and writers that have all come back to bite someone and ouch, does it hurt.

Copyright

. . . .

TAKE THE TIME—SAVE YOUR BUTT

Save your butt—take the time to copyright and protect your intellectual property, period. Theft is one of the real problems facing everyone in the music industry today. I mean Internet pilfering is really trying to kill the music industry. There are so many issues confronting the record industry each and every day. Since 1999, it was the old Napster, then KaZaA, and all the other ones popping up left and right.

They just can't be allowed to succeed in selling their banner ads by way of putting the record industry out of business. The Industry will survive. The accountants at the major labels will bring around costs, and executives that negotiated their huge contracts during the 90s techno-bust will have come and gone or will be salaried within the realm of sanity. The number one thing you can do is to secure your copyright for each and every song you write. Don't just send a copy to yourself registered mail and not open it. This is not valid. Make it legal from the beginning.

Start a publishing company for your songs. Assign them to this publishing company and sign yourself as a writer to your own publishing company. Tie yourself up to yourself, what an idea! It could become a leveraging point in a negotiation with a label or publishing company later. Spend the few bucks today to copyright every one of your compositions.

WHAT'S AN INDUSTRY TO DO ABOUT PIRATING?

A very dear friend of mine who is a great producer/ engineer sent me an e-mail the other day when we got into it regarding illegal downloading.

He said, "Most of those stealing don't know that it's illegal or they just don't care. The industry should haul another couple of thousand crooks to court and publicize it in a big way. No, not the big crooks, the 17-year-olds, or the 25-year-old junior executive at some big corporation. All it says on a CD is: 'All Rights Reserved' 'Unauthorized duplication is a violation of applicable laws.' Like some kid is going to know what this means. Unlike on videos or DVDs where it states the penalty a little more plainly, like 'FBI WARNING.' Maybe on a CD it should read 'If you copy and give this music to your friends, you can go to jail!' or 'Enjoy Your Five Year Vacation Behind Bars' and include a picture of their future 'boyfriend.' Ignorance of the law is no excuse for committing a crime; it hasn't worked like that in the past, why should it work like that now?"

Well said and very distinct, in my opinion. If the enforcement agencies would stop trying to be so politically correct and break the back of the pirates we could focus on making music and not appearing on panels, testifying on Capitol Hill, putting more money in the hands of lawyers—I could go on forever. It's all about greed and not about the art anymore. When I say enforcement agencies I really mean the FBI, the ones that have the big red screen warning on every DVD. Come on Capitol Hill and the courts—let those weird guys in sunglasses, trench coats and badges do their jobs, then we'll go after illegal payola! Uh wait, there's another nudge nudge, wink wink.

Let's try to change all this in the coming years. We do have the power if we become committed. I'm preaching about this because it is your road to success and don't let anyone or any dot com take that away from you. The payoff is a big part of the dream. You can't come up with your rent if there is no revenue from your work. You can't put food on the table if everything you've done is stolen from you. The enforcement of your right to profit from your work and art is the reason I advocate so much, protect yourself whenever and wherever you can.

INTELLECTUAL PROPERTY RIGHTS (IT'S YOUR REWARD)
Some say "It's so convenient to just download" well maybe it is, but if the record companies can't profit by releasing product then why should they pay out a bunch of money to us to create new product? This file sharing P2P predicament is hideous. I've seen 50% of the people I know who worked in the record industry lose their jobs in the last four years and this is only the beginning. No, the industry can't blame everything on downloading and shared files, but it is definitely at the bottom of this decline. The Courts have enough stuff to deal with in our society. Should they really be burdened with this "petty" theft? Yes, they should since if someone steals a few pennies here and a few pennies there, when it's all added up, its billions of dollars each year, in fact they think that it's in the area of 30 to 40 billion.

For all the public confusion, a long series of court rulings has made it very clear that it's against the law both to upload and download copyrighted music without permission. The US courts have consistently ruled that P2P and other unauthorized uploading and downloading inherently amounts to copyright infringement and therefore constitutes a crime.

Critics of the position the industry is taking say we're looking at our customers as the enemy, well, we're not. The customer who legally downloads or makes a copy just for himself is not who we as an industry are talking about. We love fans of the music we create, we love the acceptance it brings, we love being able to go into the studio and create more music. Let's find a way to work

with the fans and the labels to embrace downloading
from legal sites.

Currently Apple Computer Corporation has a great
site where consumers can download AAC files for their
iPod. Downloading at $0.99 a song is a realistic and well
thought out idea. During the first two years they sold
over half a billion songs via legal downloading. So you
could best say that this site is doing very well. Now let's
see how the royalty participation of IP recipients plays
out; it may get pretty litigious.

Sound Exchange (a royalty licensing/collection
agency for webcasting), Low Earth Orbit Satellite
broadcasting, and digital cable broadcasting royalties
are currently amassing a huge database for collection
and dispersion of funds to the IP participants. This is a
start and will be a factor in the future. Make sure you
go to their web site, fill out the forms, and return them
to get into the database. Maybe 10 years from now it
will amount to something. Currently it's about $0.0047
per play divided between the IP owners (50% record
company, 50% artist, writer, sometimes producer and
engineer). This is strictly a numbers game where if you
have a great song and a great performance, you get a lot
of plays. Over a year it can add up to a significant number, the more titles you have the greater the payout.
*There are many things happening right now to guarantee
the value of music to protect and reverse the rampant IP
theft. Look to the NARAS site* www.whatsthedownload.
com *or* www.musicunited.org *to keep up to date with all
the issues. Music United states recently "In one month, 243
million files were illegally dowloaded from P2P services.
The explosion in illegal copying is affecting the entire
music community. And contrary to what some people
would tell you, it's having a very real and harmful impact
on countless musicians, songwriters, and performers—*

virtually everyone, from recording engineers to record-store clerks, who dreams about making a living providing music to the public." So as a last reminder take some time, cover your butt, and file those copyrights.

CHAPTER 11

Finally

Finally That's Over

Now that you've read about all the things that go into a hit record and the fears and anxieties that will be around every corner, stop. Let's look to the good part... the music. I know that during Chapter 10 of this book you wanted to just say "Shut up, enough about downloading and stealing." Well, the end is near and I won't mention it again other than warn to you one more time to be aware of the pitfalls.

This book is supposed to be about your music, how to create it, get it into the stores, get it downloaded legally or sold off the shelves. That said, I will focus on the final issues and actions you need to take to move your career forward. There will be times when you see a brick wall ahead of you, roadblocks everywhere, and even when in the studio, self-doubts will overcome you. All of these are normal aspects of creativity. Don't despair; the answers will come to you. Just have the patience and understanding that you may not be able to do it all yourself. You may require some help, a partnership of sorts to make it through the maze just ahead.

The BIC Syndrome

I just have to state a few additional facts about working with artists, if you're a producer, engineer, or an artist yourself.

Remember those big concerts you've been to where at the end of the concert, there's 18,000 people screaming and lighting those BIC lighters or opening those cell phones, yelling out to the artist "You're the greatest." You do remember them, right? Well just think of how the artist feels when, during a 26 or so week tour, this happens to them every night. Psychologically this artist is on his way to not listening to others anymore. That's right, he thinks, "I am the greatest, how can so many people be wrong? This is a problem where no one is to blame, but still a problem that might need to be addressed. Mostly it starts to rear its ugly head on those second albums where artists come off the road with such high aspirations of greatness. You can't say anything to change this fact. You'll just soon realize that this new attitude has taken its toll.

Patience above all is the only way to settle things down in this case. Sometimes the artist will co-operate and start to see that during the past 26 weeks that not much has changed, the record sounds the same, the crowds still are buying the product, and they are just clamoring for more.

I hope you will find yourself in this predicament since it means that you're selling millions of copies of your product. Just sit back and continue to do more of the same great work that made your record sell in the first place. Write that great song and *continue* to allow others to help where needed. Move forward with little steps, to keep on top of trends, etc., but don't change everything just to change—you could lose your fan base.

Know Your Strengths

I keep harping on and on about the strength of your song and its importance. Please, for your own sake, do not trifle with this fact. To this day, all hit records were about the song. Its power to shape and influence the current generation of listeners cannot be underestimated. You do have a responsibility to your listener and to the public, as you get more and more airplay or media play. The power of this message is gigantic. Your responsibility is not just to get something on the air and in front of the listener, but also to shape the social trends of that generation. It's true; music does have that much power. To utilize this power is your responsibility to hold very near to your heart.

The *Media is the Message* is true today just as it was a couple of decades ago. This is the time of consolidation everywhere you look. The stock market has gone down 40% to 75% depending on which index you look at. The economy is in the dumper, money is tight, musicians are having a hard time supporting their families, and writers are placing 1/10th the number of songs they were able to place just 5 years ago. Producers are not getting the advances they once did, bands are not being signed. My 401K is now a 101K. I could go on and on. But through it all, the best seem to rise to the top and get heard. It's with this dream and the knowledge that it can be done, with enough hard work and talent to continue this career choice. It is all about professionalism, talent and dedication.

You know there are so many painters that struggle along until they are in their 50s and then, wow, their early works are found to be so awesome. There are great examples in music everywhere. Look to some earlier works of your favorite artist—maybe they had a depth or soul that might be missing in their later works. You must know that they try so hard to not repeat themselves that they may be missing some of the unique qualities of their earlier works. There are times when your newest works will seem to be copies of earlier works. What I'm trying to say is that sometimes we work so hard at our craft that we lose the enthusiasm and boundless raw unrestrained energy of the art.

The Final Thought

This is your music, this is your song, and this is your life's work we've been talking about. Now is the time to dedicate yourself to your art. If you're not 100% committed, then just don't bother; you'll save yourself a whole lot of time and money.

You look to the stars that have made it, look to what they had to deal with before they made it, and then decide for yourself if this is truly the path you want to take. This road is long and hard, and with so many twists and turns you'll get dizzy. But it's so much fun, so satisfying, and so all encompassing that you just can't deny it. Good luck—no, not good luck, since there is no luck here. Just go get'm' and have a great time making your music.

Appendix A

Glossary of Technical and Not So Technical Terms

3 Against 4 Phrasing: Three triplets over a four-beat bar.

12 tones: All the white and black notes in an octave on the keyboard.

A&R: Artist and Repertoire department of a record company. Usually several people within this department must like your art to get signed.

ADAT: An Alesis produced eight-track digital recorder using VHS-style tape cassettes.

Blind Rabbit and Blind Snake Joke: A blind rabbit runs into a blind snake in the forest; the rabbit says to the snake, "I wish I knew what I was." the snake moves over to the rabbit and says, "Well you're soft and furry with big floppy ears and a puff of a tail; I'd say you're a rabbit" The rabbit exclaims, "Oh thank you, thank you, now do you want to know what you are?" So the rabbit moves over to the snake and says, "Well you're slimy and have no ears, you must be an A&R man."

BPM: Beats per minute usually stated in ¼ notes per minute.

Cans: A pair of headphones used in the studio for recording with isolation.

Capacitance: In cables means the microfarads of capacity from the high side to ground—i.e., a force that resists the sudden buildup of electric voltage. Simply said, long cables can dull the sound of guitars.

CD: Compact Disc (not so technical).

CDR: Compact Disc Recordable, a CD you can "burn" at home in your computer then play in any compact disc player. There are also CD-RWs, a re-writeable compact disc format not generally suitable for music production masters.

Cheesy: Full of holes, wimpy, limburger (stinks).

Click Track: Electronic means to generate an absolutely accurate tempo guide.

Compression: A device used to reduce or squash the dynamic range of the signal passing through it.

Condenser mic: A microphone design where a condenser or capacitor is created by stretching a thin plated conductive diaphragm in front of a metal disc by positioning the two surfaces very close together; an electrical capacitor is created whose capacitance varies as the sound pressure attacks it. Any change in sound pressure causes the diaphragm to move and vibrate, which changes the distance between the two surfaces, thusly changing the capacitance. This in turn has very low mass and a much more accurate conversion of acoustic energy to electrical energy (AC).

Corner Loading: Using a corner as an acoustic amplifier for speaker cabinets (brings out the bottom end efficiency).

DA-88: A Tascam produced 8 track digital recorder using 8mm videotape style cassettes.

DAT: Digital 2 track recorder utilizing yet another size of tape in a cassette. (A lot of mechanics to pull a tiny tape across a rotating head).

Delivery Clock: Get the project done on time.

DI Box: Refers to a device that enables a musical instrument to be connected directly to a mic or line input of a mixer and provides the very high input impedance needed by most instruments.

Early Computer Files: such as Pro Tools v1.0, v2.0, v3.0 etc. or other early computer recording programs that used proprietary formats and there were a bunch of them.

EDL: Edit Decision List (electronic memory of what you did to the tracks; sooner or later you will have to flatten and decide).

Embedded: A microprocessor and DSP that is designed to do one thing and one thing only. Usually does this function with total reliability. Such as a car's electronic fuel injection… very fast boot up time, very high reliability.

EQ: A common processor used to modify the frequency response of the signal passing through it.

Expander: A processor used to increase the dynamic range of a signal passing through it.

Foldback: The term used to describe the amount of level from the live microphone directed into the headphones.

G4: An Apple computer.

G5: An even faster Apple computer.

G8: Not even thought of yet, but it will come and believe me, anything that worked on your G4 probably won't work on this!

Gain: Equals or the same as amplification… if you have 1 in and 10 out you have a gain of 10.

IDE or SCSI Drives: Hard disk drives or bulk computer storage. Treat them with respect and care.

Impedance: A measure of the complex resistive and reactive attributes of a component in an AC circuit. Simply said, the input stage of an amplifier versus the output impedance of a guitar.

Kit: It could be a drum kit or it could just be a bunch of expensive gear.

LFE: The low frequency effects channel in a surround mix. Sometimes called the dot 1 channel in a 5.1 mix.

Limiter: A device used to put an absolute ceiling on the output of the device.

Logic: Emagic's very good, very complicated sequencer and recorder program for Apple only.

Mic: Microphone.

Mic'd: How you used the Microphone in a set up... "The guitar is now mic'd."

Millisecond: 1/1000th of a second. Used as defined, the speed of sound, on a standard day, at sea level, the distance sound travels in .001 sec is about 13 inches.

Native Solution: A computer application that runs within the computer's central processor unit. Needs only some form of memory or storage.

Notation: Musical writing on a five-lined staff.

PCM: Pulse Code Modulation, a digital format used on CDs.

Phantom Power: 48 volts, DC; the positive side of the voltage rail is built out with two 6.8-kOhm resistors then fed equally to the high and low side of the incoming signal.

Phase: IN phase if a positive pulse on the capsule of a mike gives a positive pulse on pin 2 of an XLR connector.

Phase Correlation: Used in this book to refer to the ratio of on and off axis signals. Phase cancellation or destructive interference.

Proximity Effect: An increase in low frequency response of most directional cardioid mics when the source is within a couple of inches. As referred to in tight or close mic techniques.

Red Book: The format protocol for recording a CDR that will play in a normal CD player; an audio format.

RMS: Root Mean Square, or simply put, the average output of a device.

Threshold Point: The level where a device is active. Below this point the device does nothing; above this point the "gain" or working portion of the circuit is now active.

Tighten Up: Where you do a group compression of several tracks with a compressor set up to "breathe or pump."

Windscreen: Pop filter or a fine mesh screen placed in between the vocalist and the mic.

Word Clock: Computer clock frequency syncs up the samples. The synchronizing signal that indicates the sampling frequency or rate of sample words over a digital audio interface. Learn it or die, or don't use digital.

XLR Connector: A typical microphone connector with 3 pins, number 1 is Ground, number 2 is High, and number 3 is Low. But remember in England pin 3 is High.

Appendix B

Musical Frequency Chart

Sound is just air in motion—it's beaten, blown, plucked, strummed, spoken, or sung into this motion. Music or should I say sound, is a completely varied mixture of analogous vibrations created by all kinds of instruments, from a soft egg shaker to a massive kick drum.

Before you start equalizing this or that, take the time to look at the frequency range of specific instruments and note where you are positioning them within the spectrum of your mix.

Remember sound is a logarithm and the divisions along the bottom of the scale are not even. The difference on the chart between 40 and 80 Hz is one octave and it looks pretty small when in fact it is the majority of the acoustic energy, and its difference is greater than say the space between 8,000 and 15,000 Hz. The frequency scale of music (and all sound) isn't linear, but again I say, logarithmic, which is why mathematics and music often go so well together.

This chart, recreated from one designed years ago by *Stereo Review*, is very informative. It will give you an idea (if you didn't have one already) of where musical instruments lie across the audible frequency range. Look around the chart for a bit, you'll be amazed.

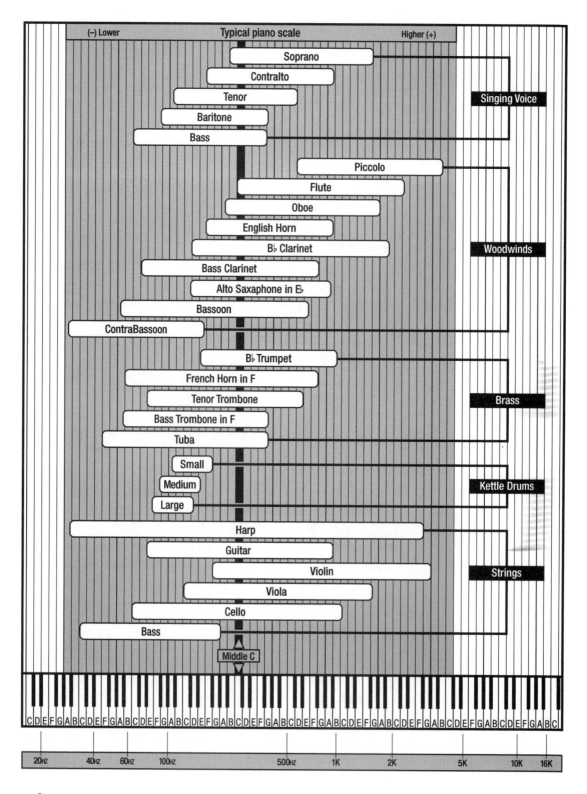

Acknowledgments

The author would like to thank the following people and organizations for their help, support, and permission to use quotes, references, and lyrics:

All the artists and record labels that had faith in my skills to allow me to spend 27 years in the studio, never getting a suntan

Jerry Wexler for his wisdom and giving me my start

Clive Davis for giving me the knowledge to know when a great song is a great song… and better not go into the studio without one

Bob Buziak for guiding me and keeping the business side so well intact

Fred Ansis, Esq. for writing great contracts that have stood the test of time

John Kolodner for being stubborn until we got it right

Billy Steinberg

Lou Gramm and Mick Jones of Foreigner

Music United Organization for their never ending energy in keeping the royalty system intact

Stevie Nicks for her friendship and honesty over the years

John Kellogg and Dolby Labs

National Academy of Recording Arts and Sciences, the P&E Wing and the Grammy Awards

Greg Mackie and everyone at Acuma Labs

All the engineers who have worked with me so well and have put up with my shit: Brian Foraker, Shay Baby, Chris Minto, Peter Love, and so many others

The RANE Corporation and the Pro Audio Reference

All the manufacturers that have taken my thoughts or opinions to heart, and in the end, come out with better products

Janice for her total support and understanding, and God only knows there have been trying times

About the Author

Born in a small town in South Dakota then moving to Minneapolis, Minnesota at the age of 12, Keith received a very Midwestern cultural education founded in reality and defined with realism. As he became more and more interested in music, both classical and pop music of the time, he was lucky enough to earn some valuable experience in a couple of the only recording studios in the Minneapolis area. Playing upright bass with light jazz bands around the University of Minnesota campus brought him into communication with many other musicians in the Twin Cities jazz, classical, and folk music scenes.

After an audition with recording artist Jimmy Rodgers for a job playing bass, Keith was hired and spent the next eight weeks on the road with Jimmy and meeting artists such as Gale Garnett, Cass Elliot, James Hendricks, Tim Rose, Felix Pappalardi, and Sean Bonniwell. Once this short eight-week tour was over, Gale Garnett asked Keith to join her folk trio and back her for a few-week stint at the Ice House in Pasadena, CA. During that engagement, Gale was signed to a record contract with RCA and a few months later "We'll Sing in the Sunshine" was a number one hit and Grammy winner and the three toured the United States with artists like the Four Seasons, Bill Cosby, Hoyt Axton, the Chad Mitchell Trio, among so many others. A wealth of soon-to-be-discovered super talents were touring and co-mingling in the folk circuit like David Crosby, Roger McGuinn, and Chris Hillman, just to name a few, where Keith could feel the energy of the oncoming change in Pop Music and Rock.

While finishing up a tour with Gale Garnett, Keith and Sean Bonniwell put their heads together and formed what turned out to be the Music Machine, a hard-rock, very tight, well-rehearsed band who had a few hits in the late 60s. During the Music Machine era, Keith met up with U of M college friend Curt Boettcher and started producing very light pop records and had success with the Association, Tommy Roe, and several others.

This collaboration and partnership caught the ear of Clive Davis, who at the time as president of CBS Records "hired" the two to produce and assist on some of the new "ambitiously electronic" sounds associated with LA bands and studios for CBS. The collaboration netted several products such as *Sweetheart of the Rodeo* by the Byrds, "At the Zoo" on the *Bookends* album by Simon and Garfunkel, and, of course, the *Millennium* album, the first 16-track album produced in America linking up two eight-track Ampex machines mechanically.

After working within the confines of CBS and IBEW union oriented studios, Keith and Curt proceeded to be named partners in a new record company venture called Together Records, a subsidiary of MGM under Mike Curb. This gave the two of them the opportunity to use outside studios, experiment with sound and more multitrack recording. Keith and Curt ended their production partnership shortly thereafter. Keith decided to move on to make sure that the individual artists' talents were always held in the highest regard. "A producer should be just a vehicle to get the artist's creativity on 'tape' in an accessible manner to the marketplace you're going after," states Keith.

In 1973, Keith wanted to fulfill his understanding of the palette available to producers by honing his engineering skills. Olsen started the production company Pogologo Productions that is still in existence and active today. The first artists he signed to Pogologo Productions were Lindsey Buckingham and Stevie Nicks, Waddy Wachtel, and Jorge Calderon. The *Buckingham Nicks* album was done first and released on Polydor Records; the next release was Waddy's single "Go to Beirut" on Anthem Records. Jorge's talent was signed to Warner Bros. Records in Burbank.

Keith sensed a change in the direction of Pop and Rock music, and spent the next 25 years as a producer and engineer helping to define it. His award-winning career is well documented by numerous websites, books, and episodes of VH1's "Behind The Music." With over 120 albums produced netting a 1 in 4 Gold or better ratio—of which more than 24 are Platinum or better, and more than 14 are multi-Platinum— sales from Keith Olsen's work exceeds 110 million units at retail, equaling more than a billion dollars in business. To date his work appears on more than 250 albums and is in many movies. Olsen has always stated, "It's about the music and how it affects the listener at home, in the car, or listening on their iPod," He adds. "Remember, we play music, we're not supposed to work at it."

Index

COURSE TECHNOLOGY

Professional ■ Technical ■ Reference

SHARPEN YOUR SKILLS, RELEASE YOUR SOUND
with these learning resources from Course Technology PTR.

The S.M.A.R.T. Guide to Mixers, Signal Processors, Microphones, and More
ISBN: 1-59200-694-9 ■ **$39.99**

The S.M.A.R.T. Guide to Recording Great Audio Tracks in a Small Studio
ISBN: 1-59200-695-7 ■ **$39.99**

The S.M.A.R.T. Guide to Digital Recording, Software, and Plug-Ins
ISBN: 1-59200-696-5 ■ **$39.99**

The Truth About the Music Business:
A Grassroots Business and Legal Guide
ISBN: 1-59200-763-5 ■ **$29.99**

The Art of Mixing:
A Visual Guide to Recording, Engineering, and Production, Second Edition
ISBN: 1-93114-045-6 ■ **$49.99**

Live Sound Reinforcement, Bestseller Edition:
A Comprehensive Guide to P.A. and Music Reinforcement Systems and Technology
ISBN: 1-59200-691-4 ■ **$49.99**

Networking Strategies for the New Music Business
ISBN: 1-59200-753-8 ■ **$24.99**

Course Technology PTR also publishes a complete offering of books, interactive CD-ROMs, and DVDs on music technology applications.

With various levels of instruction on leading software—

Pro Tools ■ SONAR ■ Home Studio ■ Cubase SX/SL ■ Nuendo ■ ACID Sound Forge ■ Reason ■ Ableton Live ■ Logic ■ Digital Performer GarageBand ■ Traktor DJ Studio ■ Soundtrack ■ and many more—

you are sure to find what you're looking for.

THOMSON
COURSE TECHNOLOGY
Professional ■ Technical ■ Reference

Visit our Web site for more information, **FREE** sample chapters, and to order.

www.courseptr.com

COURSE TECHNOLOGY

Professional ■ Technical ■ Reference

SHARPEN YOUR SKILLS, RELEASE YOUR SOUND
with these Music Technology guides!

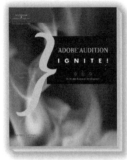

Adobe Audition Ignite!
ISBN: 1-59200-429-6 ■ **$19.99**

Pinnacle Studio 9 Ignite!
ISBN: 1-59200-475-X ■ **$19.99**

Digital Performer 4 Ignite!
ISBN: 1-59200-352-4 ■ **$19.99**

Finale 2005 Power!
ISBN: 1-59200-536-5 ■ **$29.99**

Soundtrack Ignite!
ISBN: 1-59200-428-8 ■ **$19.99**

Pro Tools LE 7 Ignite!
ISBN: 1-59200-601-9 ■ **$21.99**

SONAR 5 Power!
ISBN: 1-59200-995-6 ■ **$34.99**

Sampling and Soft Synth Power!
ISBN: 1-59200-132-7 ■ **$29.99**

How to Be a DJ
ISBN: 1-59200-509-8 ■ **$19.99**

THOMSON

COURSE TECHNOLOGY

Professional ■ Technical ■ Reference

Visit our Web site for more information and **FREE** sample chapters.
To order, call **1.800.354.9706**
or order online at **www.courseptr.com**